Woven together from true stories and testimonials gathered by the Empatheatre company, with a near-flawless presentation and delivery, *Isidlamlilo/The Fire Eater* expands our horizons, so often cramped by fears real and imagined, and imparts some of the courage the dispossessed have to gather daily to continue to live. This is fantastic theatre.

Steve Kretzmann, 2022 National Arts Festival theatre review

Through her extraordinary slow-burn incandescent performance, Mpume Mthombeni in, as, *Isidlamlilo/The Fire Eater* explores with anguish and bitter humour the quiet, desperate heroism of the African woman in the face of unrelenting suffering. It should, it will, break your heart.

Heila Lotz-Sisitka, Distinguished Professor and NRF-SARChI Chair in Global Change and Social Learning Systems Development, Rhodes University

Want to see what it means when we say theatre should be memorable, transformative, inventive, provoking, with comical nuanced shades of light and dark . . . then watch *Isidlamlilo/The Fire Eater*. It's a powerful, compelling and transformative experience.

Philisiwe Twjinstra, actor and playwright

Isidlamlilo/The Fire Eater fills a great missing space in the story of this country. It exquisitely brings to light crucial and compelling narratives about women, power and being that complicate and explain our history, all in the same entrancing performance by Mpume Mthombeni. *Isidlamlilo* is necessary and urgent viewing.

Kneo Mokgopa, Research Manager, Nelson Mandela Foundation

T0339321

Isidlamlilo / The Fire Eater

Neil Coppen and
Mpume Mthombeni

Inspired by real events

WITS UNIVERSITY PRESS

Published in South Africa by:
Wits University Press
1 Jan Smuts Avenue
Johannesburg 2001

www.witspress.co.za

First published 2024

http://dx.doi.org.10.18772/32024048790

978-1-77614-879-0 (Paperback)
978-1-77614-880-6 (Web PDF)
978-1-77614-881-3 (EPUB)

The financial assistance of the National Institute for the Humanities and Social Sciences (NIHSS) towards this publication is hereby acknowledged. Opinions expressed and those arrived at are those of the author and should not necessarily be attributed to the NIHSS.

NATIONAL INSTITUTE
FOR THE HUMANITIES
AND SOCIAL SCIENCES

Project manager: Lisa Compton
Copyeditors: Lisa Compton and Koliswa Moropa
Proofreaders: Christa Büttner-Rohwer and Koliswa Moropa
Cover design: Hybrid Creative
Typeset in 10 point Minion Pro

For Nora Mthombeni, Dudu Gumede and S
and to the Gogos of this nation, who keep
when others are prepared just to sit back a
all fall apart

Contents

Acknowledgements

We offer special thanks to the following people and organisations: the women of Thokoza Women's Hostel in Durban for sharing their stories with us; Nkanyiso and Mnqobi Mthombeni, Dylan McGarry and Kira Erwin for their love and guidance; Nomkhosi Xulu and the Urban Futures Centre researchers; Rucera Seethal and the 2022 National Arts Festival team; Dudu Gumede, Jessica Haines, Guy Buttery, Scott Marsh-Brown, Iain Robinson, Karen Logan, Tina le Roux, Aurelien Zouki, Quanita Adams, Val Adamson, and Margie and Trevor Coppen, members of the Mbazwana Creative Arts centre; Sharlene Versfeld, Sithabile Zondo, Clare Craighead and Kami Zimmer, members of the National Arts Council; Guy Nelson, Steven Woodroffe and Jackie Cunniffe; Roshan Cader and the Wits University Press team.

Foreword

ISIDLAMLILO/THE FIRE EATER:
THIS FIRE BURNS WITHIN US ALL

How do we South Africans make sense of the violence that marks our past? This play, *Isidlamlilo/The Fire Eater*, forces us to engage seriously with this question. No matter your own relationship with our violent history, this play awakens a profound and at times unsettling realisation that history is a living, breathing force in all our lives. *Isidlamlilo/The Fire Eater* is set in present-day South Africa but traverses the past as the protagonist, Zenzile Maseko, brings to life her own memories of the dying days of apartheid and the transition to democracy. Some South Africans may think they know the history of this time. Others would like to forget that history so they can pretend they are not affected by or made complicit in the events of that period. But this play is here to remind us that there are many things we do not know about our past. It reveals to us how the stories of countless black South African women can be a liberating force as we process our relationship to a violent and painful past. *Isidlamlilo/The Fire Eater* is thus a gift, an offering, a reckoning, an awakening to the discomfort and necessity of embracing the complexities of a 'history from below', a history we must sit with and with which we must coexist. We need stories like *Isidlamlilo/The Fire Eater* in order to heal. Healing stories refuse to fit into the neat versions of history that we use to justify our current actions.

Reclaiming and redressing our past through recording and making visible the histories of black South Africans and the struggle for liberation remains an important political project.[1] The project of producing history can, however, take many forms, both liberating and oppressive. Historian Noor Nieftagodien points out that the production of public history since the 1990s has focused on 'grand national[ist] narratives' that can marginalise local experiences, or only recognise their contributions to change if it serves the dominant narrative. In its 'narrower and most popular form this exercise of historical rewriting has inclined to justify the current regimes of power'.[2] *Isidlamlilo/The Fire Eater* challenges the grand narrative of what it was like to struggle against apartheid. It does so by telling an unfamiliar story woven into the familiar horror of apartheid. In this account we can no longer easily find who to blame.

Isidlamlilo/The Fire Eater is a profoundly South African story, but it resonates beyond our borders as people across the world navigate what it means to live in times of conflict. At the dawn of a new democracy emerging from the atrocities of apartheid, violent conflict between the Inkatha Freedom Party (IFP) and the African National Congress (ANC) raged in the province of KwaZulu-Natal. From the late 1980s, as the inevitable end to National Party domination was in sight, political and ethnic identities were mobilised both to resist apartheid and to galvanise the power struggle between the IFP and the ANC. This violence escalated over time, amounting to an average of 101 people killed per month between July 1990 and June 1993.[3] The reasons why politically motivated killings occurred between two organisations who opposed white domination and struggled for freedom for black people are multiple. Political sociologist Gerhard Maré identifies these as ranging from 'socio-economic conditions, to the manner in which apartheid structures created spatial and political boundaries, to direct involvement of apartheid military and police personnel, to decades of "faction fighting" in impoverished rural areas, to political policy disagreement, to the patterns of class formation, to masculinities, and much more.'[4]

What most South Africans who lived through this time remember is the sense that this conflict in KwaZulu-Natal and parts of what is today known as Gauteng was tantamount to civil war.[5] Terror and bloodshed came to rest in the most painful of ways on the doorsteps, bodies and hearts of many black families. Over two decades into our democracy the stories of this war are seldom publicly retold. The protagonist, Zenzile Maseko, was born into this violence. She becomes a woman who is both victim and oppressor, a care giver and life taker. How do we make sense of the violence that marks our past? For Zenzile the answer is simple: we survive.

As the play opens we find Zenzile, alone with her memories, in a small one-room unit in an all-women's hostel in Durban, KwaZulu-Natal's largest city. Under apartheid, black people were not allowed to live in the city, except in highly regulated hostel spaces. First established in 1923, hostels were, under colonialism and then apartheid, dormitory-like buildings run by local municipalities for black workers who provided an exploited labour force for urban industries.[6]

Hostels initially housed only men, and no families were allowed in these buildings. However, already by the 1920s, as colonial rule decimated patterns and practices of subsistence in rural areas in favour of waged labour, more and more black women came into cities looking for work.[7] Eventually women-only hostels such as the one that Zenzile lives in were built.

Hostels in South Africa are intimately wrapped up in the IFP and ANC violence of the 1990s. In greater Durban (now eThekwini municipality), some of the hostels became IFP strongholds. These hostels, particularly the large, overcrowded blocks in Umlazi and KwaMashu, became politically contested spaces where party membership and loyalty was strictly policed. Violence broke out between hostel dwellers and township residents (who were perceived to be ANC supporters). This legacy of violence lives on in a few hostels today. Under the democratic government hostels have been renamed 'community residential units' (CRUs). They remain the first port of call for many people entering cities from rural areas looking for work. Sadly, they also remain marginalised and neglected spaces in many municipalities.[8] Men's hostels have opened to families and women, a transition that has been welcomed by some residents and contested by others. The hostel that Zenzile has made her home remains a women-only hostel – a feature deeply appreciated by its residents.[9] How these socially marginalised spaces were engineered by oppressive colonial and apartheid regimes, and the way they shape life for many people migrating into the city, is excellently documented in South African literature.[10] According to Paulus Zulu, the violence in the Umlazi and KwaMashu hostels clearly shows how the 'social organisation of the hostels, marginalisation and alienation, predispose hostels to mobilisation and consequently violence on the slightest signs of provocation'. He further notes that it is important to recognise that hostel dwellers are not 'inherently aggressive, but [rather] that the social conditions that they live under make them easy prey to political manipulation'.[11]

Zenzile's story of how she becomes part of an IFP squad of women assassins is very much interwoven in these wider political tensions. What *Isidlamlilo/The Fire Eater* makes clear, however, is that Zenzile is no pawn swept along in a tide of unstoppable history. Meaningful public storytelling, such as that created by Neil Coppen and Mpume Mthombeni in this play, shows us how our own stories are always in dynamic conversation with the sociological conditions in which we find ourselves.

Isidlamlilo/The Fire Eater was inspired by the lives of real women living in a Durban hostel. These women were part of an oral history project on migration, gender and inclusion run by the Urban Futures Centre at the Durban University of Technology.[12] Oral histories were collected from thirty women. They shared their stories of arriving in the city of Durban for the first time, and of their attempts to make this place something like home. The majority of the oral history participants had travelled to South Africa from other countries in Africa. Importantly, the project also wanted to record the stories of South African women who migrated from rural areas into the city. While women have diverse experiences navigating urban life, there is much that is shared by women across these perceived national identities as they negotiate the challenges of patriarchy, capitalism, racism and other forms of discrimination.[13] From these women's oral histories we learn that hostels, while difficult living spaces with little privacy, are also places of sanctuary for some women. Desiring to move beyond just a recording of oral history,[14] the Urban Futures Centre collaborated with Empatheatre to place these stories beyond the walls of academia to ignite a public engagement that might challenge the problematic narratives around migrants and refugees in Durban. This collaboration created a powerful piece of research-based theatre, *The Last Country*, which was performed across the city in 2018 and 2019.[15]

As I have written elsewhere, I believe that 'sharing stories can change the meaning and experience of the world through reconstituting the social realm, for the storyteller and the listener'.[16] In the process of creating *The Last Country*, the oral history of one South African woman living in a hostel haunted playwrights Neil Coppen and Mpume Mthombeni. This woman related that she had served as an IFP assassin in the 1980s, a traumatic story that challenged any tidy, simplistic history of the struggle. Over the next two years I watched this story reconstitute Neil and Mpume's sense of the world. It was a story that refused to sit down and be quiet. It was a story that fascinated, troubled and expanded their understanding of our social realm. It was a story that demanded to be heard. I am very grateful that they have shared this challenging story in this beautiful play.

Through the richness and strength of women's experiences, and the way these intimate narratives are stitched into and shaped by the politics of our land past and present,

Zenzile's story is masterfully told. Flown in on the wings of the Impundulu (the lightning bird) – in Zulu folklore a shape-shifting bird associated with witchcraft and the harbinger of storms and death – Zenzile weaves her memories into a magical and terrifying tapestry. She draws on myth, religious symbolism and traditional beliefs as she shares the at times brutal, at times forgiving, realities of surviving in this land. It is a performance that touches on what it means to live with and through political violence, the transition to democracy, the brutality of inequality, epidemics such as HIV/AIDS, patriarchy and the apathetic bureaucracy of government departments. It is also the story of a remarkably formidable woman, a powerful agent in her own right, endowed with a wicked sense of humour. *Isidlamlilo/The Fire Eater* reminds us that we are seldom one thing in this world. As we walk with Zenzile through her memories, she shows us what it means to refuse to die, to refuse to be overcome.

Kira Erwin

Sociologist and Senior Researcher at the Urban Futures Centre, Durban University of Technology

Notes

1. Noor Nieftagodien, 'The Place of "the Local" in History Workshop's Local History', *African Studies* 69, no. 1 (2010): 41–61, doi: 10.1080/00020181003647181.
2. Nieftagodien, 'Place of "the Local"', 48.
3. Truth and Reconciliation Commission, 'Political Violence in the Era of Negotiations and Transition, 1990–1994', *Report of the Truth and Reconciliation Commission*, vol. 2, chap. 7, 1998,

accessed 6 September 2023, https://omalley.nelsonmandela.org/index.php/site/q/03lv02167/04lv02264/05lv02335/06lv02357/07lv02372/08lv02379.htm.

4. Gerhard Maré, 'Versions of Resistance History in South Africa: The ANC Strand in Inkatha in the 1970s and 1980s', *Review of African Political Economy* 27, no. 83 (2000): 63–79, 63, doi: 10.1080/03056240008704433.

5. Laurence Piper, 'Nationalism without a Nation: The Rise and Fall of Zulu Nationalism in South Africa's Transition to Democracy, 1975–99', *Nations and Nationalism* 8, no. 1 (2002): 73–94.

6. Hostels continue to be 'perplexing' spaces for residents. See Nomkhosi Xulu, 'From Hostels to CRUs: Spaces of Perpetual Perplexity', *South African Review of Sociology* 45, no. 1 (2014): 140–154, doi: 10.1080/21528586.2014.887919.

7. Cherryl Walker (ed.), *Women and Gender in Southern Africa to 1945* (Cape Town: David Philip, 1990).

8. See Xulu, 'From Hostels to CRUs'.

9. Angela Buckland, Jo Lees and Melinda Silverman, 'Narratives of Home and Neighbourhood: Thokoza Women's Hostel', research report for the Urban Futures Centre, 2019, accessed 6 September 2023, https://narrativesofhome.org.za/wp-content/uploads/2019/08/Narratives-of-Home-Thokoza-Womens-Hostel.pdf.

10. See, for example, Mamphela Ramphele, *A Bed Called Home: Life in the Migrant Labour Hostels of Cape Town* (Cape Town: New Africa Books, 1993), and Nomkhosi Xulu-Gama, *Hostels in South Africa: Spaces of Perplexity* (Pietermaritzburg: University of KwaZulu-Natal Press, 2017).

11. Paulus Zulu, 'Durban Hostels and Political Violence: Case Studies in KwaMashu and uMlazi', *Transformation* 21 (1993): 1–23, 22.

12. For more information on the project, see https://durbanmigration.org.za/.

13. Kira Erwin and Monique Marks, 'The Economic Lives of Migrant Women in a South African City: Informal Work, Gender, and Transformative Possibilities', *Third World Thematics: A TWQ Journal* 7, nos. 4–6 (2022): 262–282.

14. Koni Benson and Richa Nagar, 'Collaboration as Resistance? Reconsidering the Processes, Products, and Possibilities of Feminist Oral History and Ethnography', *Gender, Place & Culture* 13, no. 5 (2006): 581–592.
15. Kira Erwin, 'Storytelling as a Political Act: Towards a Politics of Complexity and Counter-hegemonic Narratives', *Critical African Studies* 1, no. 3 (2021): 237–252.
16. Erwin, 'Storytelling', 2, drawing on Michael Jackson, *The Politics of Storytelling: Variations on a Theme by Hannah Arendt*, vol. 4 (Copenhagen: Museum Tusculanum Press, 2013).

Notes on the script and staging

Isidlamlilo/ The Fire Eater is a lengthy monologue performed by the play's protagonist, Zenzile Maseko, who remains on stage throughout the show's ninety-minute duration. While there are various other characters featured throughout the story, all of them are portrayed and voiced by Zenzile during her conversation with Nkulunkulu (God).

The play is largely in English with a number of idiomatic phrases and descriptions kept in isiZulu. Mpume Mthombeni, the actor who originated the role, is adept in language/code switching and, depending on the demographics of our South African audiences, switches the language ratio of the play each night to reach her listeners. In this text we have attempted to keep a majority of the spoken isiZulu, with footnotes providing English translations.

For the sake of clarity, the play script has been broken down into scenes and the supporting characters are given individual names such as 'Pink Nails' or 'Pastor'. It is important to note that these additional characters are all either portrayed, mimicked or embodied by Zenzile in real time. Events and actions on the stage are continuous, and the telling of the story takes place over the course of a single evening, incorporating multiple flashbacks and – in the case of the final scene – projecting the audience into the future.

All of this takes a highly skilled actor, and it is little wonder critics have cited Mpume Mthombeni's solo performance as a theatrical tour de force. Throughout the play, Zenzile morphs into a range of characters, including a Home Affairs official, a pastor, schoolchildren and churchgoers, as well as multiple versions of her past self, aged five to fifty.

In the original staging of the production, shifts in the actor's voice and physicality, minimal but effective costume changes, evocative soundscapes, subtle lighting transitions and musical underscoring allowed this to happen both cinematically and seamlessly without distractions or blackouts in between.

The transitions between time frames and characters are intentionally fluid and should never impede the play's storytelling momentum as Zenzile moves between the conversational present and her memories of the past. During performances it is crucial that audiences are able to orient themselves in the story chronologically, and once again costume, lighting, sound design and recurring musical motifs help to achieve this.

The play is designed to occupy a small performance space so that the audience members feel they are sitting alongside Zenzile in her claustrophobic hostel room. As much as Zenzile is engaged in an unfolding conversation with Nkulunkulu (God), her monologue is at the same time an intimate conversation with the audience, and we believe that the more minimal the distance between performer and spectator, the more deeply and profoundly this exchange will be felt.

Neil Coppen
4 July 2023

Figure 1: Set designer Greg King and director Neil Coppen placed the *Isidlamlilo/The Fire Eater* set at a dramatic angle and removed parts of walls, enabling audiences to become intimate witnesses to Zenzile Maseko's story. The angled surfaces afforded lighting designer Tina le Roux the opportunity to cast shadows of falling rain and Zenzile's many shadow selves across the room. (*Photograph by Val Adamson. Elizabeth Sneddon Theatre, Durban, 2022.*)

Figure 2: The remarkable Mpume Mthombeni co-developed and performed the character of Zenzile Maseko. Throughout the play Mthombeni shape-shifts into a cast of characters, including a Home Affairs official, a pastor, schoolchildren and churchgoers, as well as multiple versions of her past self, age five to fifty. (*Photograph by Val Adamson. Elizabeth Sneddon Theatre, Durban, 2022.*)

Figure 3: In the latter years of her life, and after suffering a debilitating stroke, Zenzile turns to Nkulunkulu (God) in the hope of cleansing herself of her past sins, only to be rejected by the congregation of her church when they recognise her as the feared assassin Impundulu (the lightning bird). In Scene 12, 'Resurrection', Mpume Mthombeni delivers a rousing sermon as Pastor Mazibuko. Through scenes such as these, playwrights Coppen and Mthombeni expand on the central concerns of the play, which explore ideas around redemption, rebirth and forgiveness. (*Photograph by Val Adamson. Elizabeth Sneddon Theatre, Durban, 2022.*)

Figure 4: Zenzile recounts the moment when a group of ANC men kidnap her and leave her for dead at the eTafuleni Cemetery (Scene 11, 'The fall of Impundulu'). During this harrowing scene, Zenzile is unpacking her laundry basket and a crumpled green dress becomes a stand-in for her broken body during the traumatic incident. (*Photograph by Val Adamson. Elizabeth Sneddon Theatre, Durban, 2022.*)

Figure 5: In Scene 8 ('The rise of Impundulu'), Zenzile uses her walking stick to take aim while relaying the story of how she was recruited into the Inkatha Freedom Party as the assassin nicknamed Impundulu. (*Photograph by Val Adamson. Elizabeth Sneddon Theatre, Durban, 2022.*)

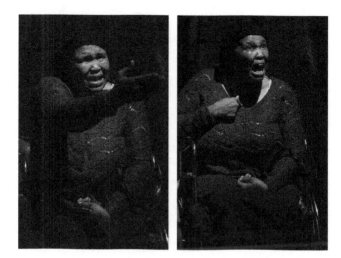

Figures 6 and 7: After Home Affairs mistakenly declare her dead and are unable to reverse the error on their system, Zenzile finds herself cast into a Kafkaesque nightmare, forced to reawaken and embrace the vengeful spirit of Impundulu (the lightning bird) in an attempt to secure her survival. Zenzile's absurd and tragic situation is based on actual stories of South African women who mistakenly have been declared dead by Home Affairs and, in many instances, were made to wait for over a decade for the error to be reversed. (*Photograph by Val Adamson. Elizabeth Sneddon Theatre, Durban, 2022.*)

Figures 8 and 9: In a review of *Isidlamlilo/The Fire Eater* for the *Daily Maverick*, writer Kneo Mokgopa commented: '*Isidlamlilo* fills a great missing space in the story of this country. It exquisitely brings to light crucial and compelling narratives about women, power and being that complicate and explain our history, all in the same entrancing performance by Mpume Mthombeni.' (*Photograph by Val Adamson. Elizabeth Sneddon Theatre, Durban, 2022.*)

Figures 10 and 11: *Isidlamlilo/The Fire Eater* plays with religious symbols, numerology and myth, and in many ways Zenzile's story can be read as a subversive reimagining of the Adam and Eve story from the Old Testament. The story begins with false accusations of witchcraft laid against her as a child, rumours which see her expelled from her Garden of Eden. By the end of the play, after Zenzile has outlived the apocalypse and is the only human left on earth, she takes it on herself to return to Ipharadesi and plant her grandmother's monkey apple tree back in the ground to start the world again. Zenzile ends her monologue in Scene 16 ('Peace') having literally tamed the feared imfezi (cobra), stroking it while it lies curled up contentedly on her lap like a fat cat. (*Photograph by Val Adamson. Elizabeth Sneddon Theatre, Durban, 2022.*)

Figure 12: In the final image of the play, the lightning scar projected on Zenzile's back is mirrored by the tree sapling placed centre stage. The scar is used throughout the play to explore the vestiges of trauma and violence that mark the bodies and lives of many South Africans. While some characters in the play chose to interpret the scar as an evil omen – 'the wings of the lightning bird' – Zenzile's grandmother is able to transform this painful mark into a symbol of regeneration and strength, referring to it as 'a river getting stronger and stronger with many, many smaller streams flowing into it . . . the tree of all life'. (*Photograph by Val Adamson. Elizabeth Sneddon Theatre, Durban, 2022.*)

Production credits

Produced by Empatheatre in association with the 2022
National Arts Festival
Featuring Mpume Mthombeni as Zenzile Maseko
Directed by Neil Coppen
Written by Neil Coppen and Mpume Mthombeni
Lighting design by Tina le Roux
Sound design by Tristan Horton
Set design by Greg King
Additional set dressing by Dylan McGarry, Neil Coppen
and Wendy Henstock
Production management by Tina le Roux/Guy Nelson
Rain SFX by Steven Woodroffe
Poster design by Dylan McGarry
Stills photography by Val Adamson

Isidlamlilo/The Fire Eater first premiered at the Rhodes Box
Theatre in Makhanda, South Africa, on 1 July 2022 as
part of the 2022 National Arts Festival main programme.

Scene 1

CONVERSATIONS WITH NKULUNKULU

As the audience enters, they encounter sixty-something ZENZILE MASEKO *sitting in her concrete cube of a room in a downtown Durban women's hostel.*

The space is cramped. When ZENZILE *rises from the bed, she needs only to hobble a few paces before she has reached the kitchen counter situated on the opposite side.*

Outside, rain can be heard falling from the gutters . . . the occasional rumble of thunder . . . distant street and city noises . . . hooting cars . . . tyres slushing through puddles . . . the whistles of taxi drivers . . . and conversations of street vendors as they pack up for the night.

ZENZILE *sits on the edge of her bed, shoes cast aside, rubbing her swollen ankles. A wheelchair sits beside the bed. Since her stroke,* ZENZILE *has lost the use of her right hand and has been largely relegated to this chair. While she is able to walk short distances with the aid of a walking stick, trips outside of the hostel are undertaken with the aid of this chair.*

ZENZILE *is framed by a large window. The sickly urine-yellow sodium of a nearby street light spills into the room, casting long shadows. On the window ledge sits a framed picture of a young man, a wireless radio (with Zulu gospel music playing) and a small clay pot with a tree sapling planted in it.*

1

ZENZILE's *single bed, relegated to one corner of the room and raised on bricks, is adorned with frilly sheets and a patterned blanket folded neatly at the end. At the head of the bed stands a rusty locker, with a suitcase, blankets (still kept in plastic carry bags) and a laundry basket all balancing precariously on top.*

On a section of the wall closest to the bed are a myriad of photographs depicting ZENZILE's *family members at ceremonies and special occasions. Extending along this same wall is a washing line with items of clothing pegged all along it. A makeshift bedside table (plastic beer crate) features an isiZulu Bible sitting pride of place on top of a doily.*

Across from the bed, and at the opposite end of the room, is a waist-high cupboard which stands in for a kitchen counter, housing an electrical stove grid, cooking pots, a kettle, tin mugs and a bowl filled with a few mismatched vegetables. A bag of oranges hangs off a hook on one side of the cupboard.

As the house lights dim, ZENZILE *clasps her Bible in her hands and casts her eyes up towards the ceiling as if searching for something. When she finally speaks, it is to Nkulunkulu, God himself.*

ZENZILE: Uyazi, Nkulunkulu,[1] it's been over two years now since that girl at the Home Affairs told me I was dead. Two years. Angiqambi amanga.[2]

---

[1] You know, God

[2] I never lie.

You remember how I noticed that there was funny businesses happening? The bank closed all my accounts and my SASSA grant stopped being paid at the end of each month. My grandchild Nqobile explained to me there must be a problem with my ID and that we needed to visit the Home Affairs to sort this matter out.

Scene 2

HOME AFFAIRS SHOWDOWN (PART 1)

ZENZILE *pushes the wheelchair downstage centre before taking a seat and describing her interaction with a Home Affairs worker (referred to as* PINK NAILS*) whom she imagines is sitting in front of her. Throughout this scene* ZENZILE *relays events from memory, jumping between playing herself and* PINK NAILS *in conversation. Lighting isolates the scene from the more general setting of the hostel room.*

ZENZILE [*remembering*]: That child, chewing gum, looked up from her computer while tapping her keyboard with long pink nails.

PINK NAILS: I'm afraid, Mrs Maseko, we are unable to help you.

ZENZILE: Ngobani?[1]

PINK NAILS: Our system is saying you are deceased.

ZENZILE: Angizwanga?[2] [*Beat.*] 'Deceased,' said this girl again, as if it was a normal thing for this child to be sitting there and speaking with isipoki![3]

'Ufile,[4] Gogo!' my grandchild Nqobile repeated. 'Their system is saying you are dead!'

Hayibo,[5] dead? For how long have I been this way?

---

[1] Why not?

[2] Excuse me?

[3] a ghost

[4] You are dead

[5] an expression of shock or surprise; 'Wow'

PINK NAILS [*tapping lethargically on her keyboard with a single finger*]: It says here, um . . . um, for eleven years now.

ZENZILE [*laughs maniacally*]: Then I laughed. A laugh so loud that all of the people in that place turned to see what was happening. [*Back to speaking to* PINK NAILS.] Hayibo, wentombazane![6] But I'm right in front of you! How does this work, eh? Ngife ngiphila?[7]

PINK NAILS: It says here on my system that you died of natural causes in uMzimkhulu eleven years ago.

ZENZILE [*shocked*]: Hayibo! I've never been to uMzimkhulu even once when I was still alive . . . Tell me why, child, why would I decide to take a holiday there when I'm dead?

PINK NAILS [*tapping at her itchy weave with the side of her hand*]: I'll lodge a complaint here on the system to say that it has confused you with someone else. [*Beat.*] You know, Ma, you're not the first person this mix-up is happening to.

ZENZILE: Wooooh, from then on I let Nqobile do the talking ngoba ngase ngizwa ukuthi ikhanda lami liyagxabha ke manje.[8] Yah, that child was very lucky that, in my old age, I've learnt to control my anger or else she would have met a very different person that day. [*Beat.*] Pink Nails told my grandchild they would phone us to come back once the matter has been resolved at the head

---

[6] Wow, girl!

[7] I'm dead but I'm alive?

[8] because my head was getting too hot

office. So we went back to the hostel and waited for her call.

Lighting fades on the downstage space as ZENZILE *rises, returns the wheelchair to its corner and slumps back on her bed.*

Scene 3

IPHARADESI LOST

ZENZILE *continues her conversation with Nkulunkulu.*

ZENZILE: Ufile?[1] . . . Dead? . . . Mina?[2] Can you imagine?
[*Chuckles derisively.*] No, that child didn't know me,
Nkulunkulu. If she did, she would have known she
can't get rid of me that easily. And now what, eh? What
must I do? My grant money was no longer coming.
How was I going to eat? Pay my rent here? How was
I going to send money to Dudu, who still lives there
in Ipharadesi[3] and is helping me to finish my house?
You remember, I'm rebuilding a two-room in the rural
areas where I was born, but that house, that house of
mine hayi bandla ayipheli.[4]

Especially now with these rains you have been
punishing us with, Nkulunkulu . . . eish, they
say those floods washed away half of my house.
That's why I turn to you each night, Nkulunkulu,
and I beg you . . . please, Nkulunkulu . . . please
just switch off those taps in the sky . . . please,
Nkulunkulu, grant me the strength to return
home now and finish building my house.

---

[1] Dead?

[2] Me?

[3] Paradise

[4] is never finishing

For too many years I waited on that list for a RDP[5]
house . . . twenty years. Angiqambi amanga.[6]
No, I couldn't wait any longer. Yah, I've seen too
many people waiting their whole lives and it never
happens.

Before this, I was sending Dudu money at the end
of the month so she could buy bricks and get her
sons Dumisane and Sizwe to lay them for me. I was
making my beadwork and selling my bracelets
laphaya ebeachfront.[7] With the money I was
making, I was paying off those bricks one by one.
My social grant money was also helping, but after
the Home Affairs told me I was deceased, I haven't
been able to send anything for a long time.

Ey, Nkulunkulu, it's difficult for me to visit
Ipharadesi to go and see the work Dudu's boys
are doing on my house. [*Beat.*] It's expensive to
travel all that way in the taxi and the floods have
washed away the road. Now I would have to travel
for many hours in a taxi and get off at Mayesweni
and catch another taxi and then ask Dumisani
to push me in his wheelbarrow to the top of that
hill. The path to my house is very steep. Hayi,
Nkulunkulu. [*Chuckling.*] You would need to

---

[5] Reconstruction and Development Programme (a government
programme providing housing to the poor)
[6] I never lie.
[7] there at the beachfront

grant that boy the strength of an ox to get me to the top.

Growing up in my father's house at the top of that hill, nothing was ever straight. No, Nkulunkulu, angiqambi amanga.[8] Things could never ever keep still. Uyabona laphayana[9] you'd put a bowl on this side of the table and you would find it on the opposite side before you had a chance to put your spoon in. Angiqambi amanga![10]

My daughter Thuthukile[11] ucabanga ukuthi ngiyahlanya[12] for wanting to go back and live on that cursed hill. She says 'Yini?[13] . . . Yini, Ma? Why do you want to return to a place where so many bad things happened to you as a child?' [*Beat.*] But what other choice do I have, eh? That is the only plot of land I own . . . It's the soil of okhokho bami.[14] Where would I find the money now to buy another plot?

Thandeka, who lives in room 222 in this same hostel, has family members still staying out there

---

[8] I never lie

[9] You see, in that place

[10] I never lie!

[11] The name Thuthukile loosely translates as 'has become a better person'

[12] she thinks I'm mad

[13] Why?

[14] my ancestors

by Ipharadesi. She tells me many things have
changed. The government moved many people
away from their houses to build factories on
the one side and a rubbish dump on the other.
Now she says you can't even go down to the
river. You can't swim or wash anymore in those
pools where Musa and I used to play as children.
Ngiyakutshela![15]

Yah, when I was a girl Musa and I were friends
. . . That one was like a brother to me. He was the
child belonging to our neighbours, the Bophelas
. . . we were the same age. Wooooh, we used to
play too much together . . . splashing in that water
and climbing the isihlahla samahlala[16] tree to
break open those monkey apples[17] and eat the soft
fruit in the middle until our stomachs hurt. But
when our fathers began to fight over the grazing
territories, uma wami[18] told me I must stop
playing with him. [*Beat.*] Things got very tense
between our families . . . but children don't care
about big people's politics . . . no . . . no . . . no . . .

---

[15] I'm telling you!
[16] Zulu name for the monkey apple tree (*Strychnos
madagascariensis*), which can be found in open woodland, on
rocky koppies, and in riverine and coastal forests throughout
southern Africa
[17] Monkey apples are a soft fruit encased in a hard calabash-like
shell.
[18] my mother

They just make a plan to carry on away from the eyes of their elders. Yah, bayaqhubeka nje bona[19] . . . Musa and I . . . we carried on.

But now Thandeka says the children don't go near that river anymore. She says the fish are all dead . . . the water is oily and stinking . . . you can't drink from it . . . you can't wash . . . Ungathi ufaka izimpahla zakho ku Jik. Uyacabanga?[20] And the smell from the dump! Wooooh weeeee, she says the people must sleep with their windows closed so that the smell doesn't creep in like a thief in the night to disturb them. [*Beat.*] Not many people live out there anymore. Dudu says just about the only thing still living on that hill in Ipharadesi are the imfezis[21] . . . the amacobras. Wooooh, there are many snakes living in those bushes around my house, uyangizwa?[22] Angiqambi amanga![23] Big, big ones. Fat ones. And that thing that they call . . . What is this animal? . . . It's like a wild dog that bites and is very dangerous. The children chased them into the bushes with stones when they were puppies because they were born

---

[19] they just carry on

[20] It's like dipping your clothes in Jik (bleach), she says. Can you imagine?

[21] cobras

[22] you hear me?

[23] I never lie!

funny, yabona nje[24] . . . with missing legs and
eyes and whatnot . . . and there, hiding in those
bushes, those dogs grew very wild again. Yah,
they caught that disease that made them want
to bite everything they set eyes on . . . lesasifo
senza ukuthi kube sengathi bezixubha amazinyo
ngomuthi wamadoda wokushefa intshebe . . .
kuyabila nje amagwebu![25]

When I was little, ubaba wami[26] would tease me,
saying that if I behaved badly, lezazinja zasendle[27]
would come into my room at night and think
that my toes were sausages. [*She unfolds a nearby
blanket and covers her legs, making sure her toes
don't peek out the bottom.*] Can you imagine?
Ngiyakutshela![28] For a long time those dogs chased
me in my nightmares. [*Beat.*] Kuze kube imanje,
Nkulunkulu, ngisalala ngezinyawo ezigoqwe
ngoblanket.[29]

*She begins massaging her weak hand, while gazing
longingly out the window, as if Ipharadesi exists on
the other side of the pane.*

---

[24] you see

[25] that sickness (rabies) that made them look like they were
brushing their teeth with the man's shaving cream . . . bubbling
foam!

[26] my father

[27] wild dogs

[28] I'm telling you!

[29] To this day, God, I still sleep with my feet under the blanket.

ZENZILE: Eish, Ipharadesi. [*Lost in the memory.*] I feel a
    deep pain in my heart when the women from this
    hostel say they are going back to visit their homes.
    When Christmas comes and everyone returns to their
    families in the rural areas, I'm left lying in this bed,
    staring at the roof, dreaming of that view from the hill
    in Ipharadesi.

You know, Nkulunkulu, I always imagine myself
    [*Chuckling.*] sitting there on the veranda of
    my new house . . . under the stars . . . drinking
    umqombothi.[30] [*She removes a scarf that has been
    draped around her neck and coils it into her lap.*]
    Sitting there with one of those imfezis curled on
    my lap like a fat cat and a wild dog snoring at my
    feet. [*Beat.*] Yah, that's where I find my peace . . .
    inside that picture . . . there beside the creatures
    who've spent their whole lives hiding in the
    shadows.

Weh, Nkulunkulu, you see these? [*She rolls up
    her sleeves and shows bite marks.*] These are
    from the teeth of an imfezi. Yah, you remember,
    Nkulunkulu? I was bitten while collecting
    firewood in the forest near my husband
    Bangizwe's house . . . the house we lived in
    before we moved to Lindelani. You can see for
    yourself. [*Gesturing towards the scars.*] Angiqambi

---

[30] traditional Zulu beer

amanga.[31] When I got back home Bangizwe was looking at me with big eyes. He told me, 'Ai, Zenzile, we must call an ambulance or you will be dead by the morning' . . . but I just laughed and carried on preparing our dinner.

That night Bangizwe kept shaking me in our bed, pushing me with his finger to see if I was still breathing. Eventually I just laughed and said, 'Hayi, suka wena[32] . . . What must happen? Do you really think an imfezi can kill me when not even the lightning could?' [*Beat.*] No, Lord, after that night my husband respected me afresh. He never again hit me after his drinking because he knew . . . he knew . . . that if I wanted to, I would beat the hell out of him back!

---

[31] I never lie.
[32] Hey, get out of here

Scene 4

IMPUNDULU STRIKES

A rumble of thunder outside as the storm begins to circle back.
As rain patters down, ZENZILE *shuffles towards the stove,*
keeping her eye on the building storm.

ZENZILE: In the summer, Nkulunkulu, your rains came.
  They would turn those valleys in Ipharadesi into
  rivers of mud. [*Chuckling.*] Ugogo wami wayehlezi
  ethi uma kufika izimvula, lezantaba zazimila imilenze
  zibaleke.[1] [*Beat.*] We thought we would always be safe
  in that home. Umkhulu wami wayewakhile lowamuzi.
  Wawukotele ubambelele ngezinzipho entabeni and
  awukaze nakanye unyakaze.[2]

  She puts a battered old kettle on the stovetop and
  switches it on. Rain intensifies outside.

ZENZILE: Ugogo wami[3] only told me many years later that
  a story in the newspaper said that when the lightning
  struck our home, it was so bright and hot that it
  melted all the spoons, knives and forks in the kitchen
  drawers. Angiqambi amanga.[4] When the police arrived

---

[1] My grandmother used to say that when the rains came, those hills
liked to grow legs and run away with themselves.

[2] My grandfather had built that house very strong. It clung to the
side of that hill by its fingernails and never once let go.

[3] My grandmother

[4] I never lie.

and turned that drawer upside down, a big block of metal fell out on the ground. I'm telling you, I still get headaches . . . even to this day . . . The light still hurts my eyes.

Music begins merging with the sounds of the storm. Hot white lightning flashes outside the window. ZENZILE *clutches a pillow and revisits the scene.*

ZENZILE: I should have buried my face in my pillow . . . turned away . . . but it was too powerful. That big, big bird . . . a demoni[5] stretching out its wings of burning white feathers inside our room. Its tail was the green-blue colour of the sky . . . umlomo nezinyawo kubomvu tebhu njengomlilo ovuthayo.[6] I watched as it flew through the house saying nothing but touching everything: tin . . . walls . . . thatch . . . skin.

The lightning flashes now appear to be moving inside the room. Rain rushes down the windowpane, subterranean shadows streaking across ZENZILE'S *face. Her expression is a mixture of horror and awe.*

ZENZILE: Then it went dark and silent. [*Beat.*] I remember the smell of burnt hair . . . the feeling of boiling water being poured down my back.

---

[5] demon
[6] beak and legs licked red with fire

Pause. The storm retreats and subsides. In the silence a soft morning light breaks through the window.

ZENZILE: When the sun rose, I saw uma wami[7] lying in her bed, her mouth open, hands shielding her face, fingers curled like the claws of a sparrow . . . and ubaba wami,[8] his skin rough and shiny like charcoal. [*She lights a match and watches the flame reach towards her fingers.*] Elele laphaya sengathi umentshisi ovuthe washa kwaze kwayofika ezansi.[9]

After that I moved into my gogo's house. Impilo yami yashintsha lapho ke.[10] [*Beat.*] When Musa and I next went to swim at the river, I took off my dress, but that one, he refused to follow me in. He just stood there . . . umlomo wakhe ulenga[11] . . . pointing at my back, before crying all the way back up the hill to his mother's house.

---

[7] my mother
[8] my father
[9] Lying there like a match that had been burnt right down to the bottom of the stick.
[10] My life was never the same after that.
[11] his mouth by his belly button

Scene 5

THE SCAR

ZENZILE *takes on the role of* GOGO *in this scene. As the scene opens,* ZENZILE *sits on the edge of her bed.*

ZENZILE: I remember how ugogo wami[1] used a wet cloth to cool the scars that the lightning bird had scratched into my back.

She retrieves a wet cloth and mimes the action of her grandmother cooling her scar with the cloth, dabbing cold water tenderly across it. Lighting shifts to isolate the scene and the dialogue between the two characters.

GOGO: Shhh . . . shhh, ngane yami.[2]
ZENZILE [*as child*]: Kodwa kubuhlungu,[3] Gogo.
GOGO: Shhhh . . . shhhh . . . Amanzi azokupholisa.[4]
ZENZILE [*as child*]: Why is everything hurting me like this, Gogo?
GOGO: What is hurting, ngane yami?[5]
ZENZILE [*as child*]: Izinto abazishoyo,[6] Gogo.
GOGO: What are they saying?

---

[1] my grandmother
[2] my child
[3] But it hurts
[4] Let the water cool you.
[5] my child
[6] The things they are saying

ZENZILE [*as child*]: Ukuthi ngiyathakatha[7] . . . that I was
using umuthi[8] . . . that's why umama nobaba[9] are gone
and I am still here.

GOGO: Ay, and you pay attention to this nonsense?

ZENZILE [*as child*]: Musa has been telling all the others that
the morning before the lightning came, he saw me
speaking with that bird on the riverbank.

GOGO: Yiphi inyoni?[10]

ZENZILE [*as child*]: Impundulu[11] . . . the one that has a
hammer for a head.[12]

GOGO [*firmly*]: Ay, Zenzile, you must not name this thing
in my house! This creature has nothing to do with
you, ngane yami![13] Nothing! It only has an appetite for
destruction. Wherever it lands it guides the lightning
there. [*Beat.*] Umtshele uMusa ukuthi uzoba nesibazi
esingaphezu kwesakho esinqeni uma eqhubeka
nokuhamba eqamba amanga.[14] Ngeke ngiwubekezelele
mina ushidi.[15]

---

[7] That I'm a witch

[8] witchcraft and evil spells/medicine

[9] my mother and father

[10] Which bird?

[11] the lightning bird (a shape-shifting bird endowed with demonic
powers in Zulu folklore)

[12] The hamerkop (*Scopus umbretta*) is believed by many to be the
lightning bird (Impundulu).

[13] my child

[14] You must warn Musa that he will have a scar far bigger than
yours across his backside if he carries on spreading these lies.

[15] I don't tolerate nonsense.

ZENZILE [*as child*]: How do I wash away their lies, Gogo? . . .
How do I make sure this bird never visits me again?

GOGO: There's little you can do to destroy this idemoni.[16] If
you try, it only comes back stronger than before. No,
you cannot shoot it or stab it . . . drown or even poison
it. The only way to kill it is by fire! [*Beat.*] But I know
a secret which I must share with you, ngane yami. The
only way you can let this creature inside to make a
messy nest of your heart is by letting the fire of their lies
consume you. Qaphela,[17] Zenzile . . . be careful, ngane
yami, not to become the stories others tell about you!

ZENZILE [*narrating while demonstrating the action*]: Then
Gogo traced her cloth along the pattern on my back.

GOGO [*tenderly, almost in a whisper*]: No . . . no . . . no, these
marks are not the wings of idemoni. That's not what
I see at all. [*Beat.*] I only see a river getting stronger
and stronger with many, many smaller streams flowing
into it. The curious, thirsty roots of a tree . . . isihlahla
sempilo[18] . . . the tree of all life. This is a blessing, not
a curse. A reminder from amadlozi[19] that death has
turned its face away from you while its cheek was still
hot. A reminder that you are still here, my child . . .
Usaphila![20]

Lights fade on the scene.

---

[16] demon
[17] Be careful
[18] the tree of life
[19] your ancestors
[20] You are still here!

Scene 6

ZENZILE'S FIRST REVENGE

In this scene ZENZILE *plays herself as well as taking on the voices of her childhood friend* MUSA *and his friends.*

ZENZILE: But the stories people were telling got so bad that my gogo kept me from going back to school for many weeks. When I finally did, you would never believe what those boys did to me there! Ai, ai, ai, Nkulunkulu, kubuhlungu uma ngicabanga loluyasuku.[1]

A rumble of thunder. The musical underscore takes a darker turn.

ZENZILE: They caught me in the playground . . . pushed me into the toilet and pinned me down. The other children were crowding around. Musa was at the front telling them each to pay him fifty cents. After he collected their money he tore my shirt off. Buttons went spinning across the tiles. I stood there . . . nginamahloni[2] . . . covering my chest.

ZENZILE tears her jersey off and clutches it to her breast. As she makes this sudden movement, she turns her back to the audience. The lights dim, revealing an intricate pattern of lightning projected

---

[1] it pains me to remember that day
[2] burning with shame

and smouldering across her back. The lightning scar resembles an upside-down tree.

ZENZILE: 'Bheka . . . bheka . . . Ngangiqinisile,'[3] said Musa, pointing. 'See, I'm telling you the truth. Look how Impundulu has licked her with its tongue of fire!' 'Hayibo!' said another. 'She even wears the marks of its wings on her back.'
'Ungumthakathi,'[4] they chanted. 'She's a witch . . . Ungumthakathi . . . Ungumthakathi.'

Lights come up as ZENZILE *turns her attention skyward, ranting now at Nkulunkulu.*

ZENZILE: Why must you punish me like this, Nkulunkulu? Why must you make me stay in this ugly city for so long while my house is never finishing? Is it for those things I did in my past? [*Beat.*] Was it because I was rude? Yah, I was rude when I was younger. I used to say and do whatever was on my mind. That lightning left me with a terrible temper. My head would overheat like an old car engine and I could no longer keep my thoughts to myself . . . They would just fly off my tongue and fall on someone else's lap before I had the chance to catch them.

ZENZILE'S *focus now shifts from Nkulunkulu to the memory of* MUSA *on the road in front of her. She eyes him bitterly.*

---

[3] Look . . . look . . . I was right.
[4] She's a witch

22

ZENZILE: That same day, when I was on my way home from school, I saw Musa there walking ahead of me. Storm clouds settled over my heart. I picked up a monkey apple from the side of the road – the one with the shell as hard as a rock. I felt its weight in my hand.

Music takes a darker, discordant turn. ZENZILE *picks up the nearby cloth which her gogo used moments ago to cool her scar and scrunches it tightly into a ball.*

ZENZILE: My head getting hot . . . hot . . . hot! Seligxabha njengeketela eliyekiwe nje esitofini.[5]

The kettle boiling on the stove begins to emit a faint whistle.

ZENZILE: I called out his name . . . Musa! . . . Musa Bophela! There was a flash . . . [*Calling.*] Musa! . . . He turned . . . My monkey apple flew through the air and kissed him on the mouth. [*She lets out a roar as she lobs the scrunched cloth forcefully across the stage. At the same time she kicks a tin bowl resting at her feet. The bowl is filled with red and white Zulu beads and they scatter across the floor, rattling like teeth.*] He collapsed . . . blood everywhere . . . spitting out his two front teeth in the dirt.

ZENZILE *rises from the bed. Her shadow looms menacingly across the back wall. She moves centre*

---

[5] Hot like a kettle left on the stove long after its whistling.

stage, miming the action of pinning MUSA *to the
ground with her knee. The kettle on the stovetop
screeches and hisses.*

ZENZILE: Then I pushed my knee deep into his back and
said, 'The next time Impundulu strikes, she will make
sure you never get up again. Uyangizwa, Mfana?[6] . . .
Uyangizwa?' [*Beat.* ZENZILE *shrinks back from the
memory, her hulking physicality from before returning
to that of a frail older woman.*] That was the last time
I would see that boy . . . The next time we would meet
each other, he would be a grown man . . . Kodwa
leyondaba, Nkulunkulu, ngiyobuye ngiyixoxe.[7]

---

[6] Do you understand, boy?
[7] But that, Nkulunkulu, is a story for another time.

Scene 7

EXILE

ZENZILE *hobbles over to the stove and removes the boiling kettle from the heat. She pours herself a cup of tea, dunking the tea bag in and out before heaping in four spoonfuls of sugar.*

ZENZILE: The only thing I like about living in this hostel is that men are not allowed inside. No, Nkulunkulu, men cause too many problems. Ngiyakutshela![1] Wabenzelani baba nje, eh?[2] It's impossible not to be jealous when a man gives money to one woman and you don't get any. You would want that man for yourself if he was bringing in money like this. [*She sips her tea conspiratorially.*] That man would not even reach your room if he was allowed to come to visit! Yah, he would be stolen before he reaches your door, and when his girlfriend realises what has happened she would leave her room with a cooking knife to set matters right. [*Beat.*] If men were allowed to come inside here, there would be many women living here who would be dead by now. [*Chuckling.*] Wooooh weeee, Lord my Saviour, you can be certain of that!

ZENZILE *replaces the kettle with a cooking pot of water on the stovetop. She retrieves a cutting*

---

[1] I'm telling you!
[2] Why did you make them like this, eh?

knife and a bowl of potatoes and makes her way
over to the wheelchair, which is placed beside the
countertop. As she passes the window she notices a
framed picture of her husband, Bangizwe. She looks
at it fondly for a moment.

ZENZILE: I met my husband, Bangizwe,[3] when I was a
teenager and we married soon after. I only married
once. Kwakwanele nje lokho kumina.[4] [*Beat.*]
Sometimes I wonder if I married him just to escape the
house of my uncle that I was living in at the time.

It was very, very painful for my grandmother and
me to be separated, but it was no longer safe for
me to stay in Ipharadesi with her.

She sits in the wheelchair and begins peeling the
potatoes with her knife.

ZENZILE: Whenever death visited our people . . . whenever
the rains washed away their houses or lightning struck
. . . stories were whispered about how Zenzile had been
seen down by the river plotting with that lightning
bird. Eventually men from the community surrounded
Gogo's house and threatened to burn it to the ground.

I was sent to stay with my uncle in Kwa-Mashu,
but that man didn't want to share his house with a
child accused of witchcraft. Whenever he had bad

---

[3] Bangizwe translates as 'fighting for land'.
[4] That was enough for me.

luck . . . Uma elahlekelwe imali yestokofela noma eshiywe umfazi wakhe wayothandana nomunye umfazi . . . kwakuyiphutha lami[5] . . . Yah, he said it was me who was cursing him.

He never let me go back to school. Even though I was still young he put me to work. I would go around to people's houses and work in their gardens, doing whatever jobs I could find, and every cent I made he would spend on his beer.

When I was a teenager there were jobs that he made me do that were not right. No, I don't like ihlazo.[6] It's difficult for me to ever accept what happened. [*Beat.*] When I think about my life as a young woman, mina ngangenza engangikutshelwa[7] . . . I was only doing what the men told me to do.

You remember, Nkulunkulu, you sent me a baby girl, Thuthukile. I gave birth to her just before her father passed. She was too young to remember him. [*Beat.*] No, I haven't seen Thuthukile for many months. She lives there in Umlazi with her boyfriend. It's difficult for me to get along with her ngoba mina angizwani nje nomuntu

---

[5] When his wife left him for another woman or when he lost money on the stokvel . . . it was my fault.

[6] disgrace

[7] I always did as I was told

wesifazane ongalisabi ihlazo.[8] No, I don't like that at all. I found it difficult to even feel sorry for her even when I heard she was ill. I'd saved up enough money to send her to school and give her the opportunities I never had, but she failed. What did she choose instead of education, Nkulunkulu? Amadoda . . . men . . . wakhetha ukuhlala ehlazweni.[9] She even went and stayed with that boy in Umlazi without seeking my permission first. I'm telling you, she just went and lived there like that.

After I had this stroke, Thuthukile's daughter Nqobile came to live with me at the hostel, but she's hardly here anymore. When I find out where she has been hiding for the last few days there's going to be trouble. Later today I will load airtime and call her. [*She mimes the conversation on an imaginary phone.*] 'Yah, Nqobile, when you next return here, you must pack your bags now and voetsek![10] Maybe you've forgotten what kind of a person I am. Ngiyakholwa ukukholwa kodwa amasimba angizwani nawo.'[11] Yah, when she answers that phone I'll say to her, 'Ingabe kumnandi lapho?[12] I hope it is. I hope you're

---

[8] because I don't like disgrace in women
[9] She chose . . . men . . . she chose to live in disgrace.
[10] go away (Afrikaans)
[11] I believe in God but that doesn't mean I take shit from anyone.
[12] Is it nice there?

enjoying your time while I'm left to do the washing with one hand! Eating, washing and wiping my ass with one hand. Is it nice there?' [*Beat.*] How can that child relax when she knows I'm all alone here without any help? No . . . no . . . no, I'm not a relaxer, I'm not a relaxer at all. She should know that by now.

Thunder rolls outside.

ZENZILE: Bangizwe was a good man. We shared some happy years together, but he changed after he got caught up working for that IFP[13] taxi boss uNzondo. He started to stay out late, attending meetings and rallies, working over the weekends. Some nights he'd get into the bed and tell me how the ANC[14] government that was coming into power was wanting to destroy the Zulu nation. We needed to make sure that our leaders were given all the crosses when the voting time came. He used to say, 'Zenzile, I'm telling you, there's a big . . . big storm building over this nation of ours.' [*Beat.*] He wasn't wrong about that.

---

[13] Inkatha Freedom Party, a political party supported by ethnic Zulus

[14] African National Congress

Scene 8

THE RISE OF IMPUNDULU

The noise of the storm grows louder as it draws near. Lighting gradually isolates ZENZILE *in her wheelchair.*

ZENZILE: It wasn't just Bangizwe who paid that price in the end. Thousands of people died back then in the eighties. Before I always used to hear them talking about how this one or that one had been given the 'necklace',[1] but that word meant nothing to me. It was only when I saw him with that wire from the wheel burnt into his chest . . . [*She lights a match and watches it burn out.*] eshe njengomentshisi ovuthe kwaze kwayofika phansi ekugcineni kwawo[2] . . . that I understood what they meant.

Thuthukile was still a baby. We were forced to spend many nights sleeping in the bushes. Hawu! There were gangs of schoolchildren terrorising our streets with pangas and petrol bombs, and the police were doing nothing to stop them. [*Beat.*] How could you sleep peacefully in your home when this was happening outside? We used to hide in those bushes. You remember, Nkulunkulu, how I'd hold Thuthukile close to my breast, not

---

[1] People who were 'necklaced' were set alight with a car tyre hung around their neck.

[2] burnt like a match down to the very bottom of the stick

making a sound, covering her mouth with a dishcloth to make sure no one knew we were there.

Beat.

ZENZILE: After Bangizwe's death, my head became very, very hot and those wild dogs from Ipharadesi – yah, those dogs returned to chase me again in my dreams.

I knew things were about to change when I came home from Bangizwe's funeral and for the first time I saw that bird . . . the one with a hammer for its head . . . just sitting on the roof and watching me.

The next day Nzondo knocked on my door and said he wanted to speak with me. During that meeting he told me that Bangizwe had told him I was a very strong woman who didn't put up with people's nonsense. He told me he knew where each of those ANC men – the ones who had killed my husband – were hiding. Then he invited me to work for him . . . but to do this I would need to give up my old life . . . I would need to change my name.

When he asked me what I wanted to call myself, I said, without thinking, 'Impundulu! From now on, that is what the people will know me as.'

Yah, there was a good reason I named myself after this creature and didn't choose a name like 'Prudence' . . . 'Mercy' . . . or 'Forgiveness'.

The pot begins to boil over. Its lid rattles.

ZENZILE: This is a part of my life, Nkulunkulu, that – day by day – I'm trying to wash away. When I think about my life as a young woman . . . ngangenza engangikutsheliwe[3] . . . I was only doing what I was told. I was one of those women that ate fire . . . They called us Isidlamlilo.[4] We were known back then for ukuthi sasinochuku.[5] That is what we did there in the IFP.[6] We beat the hell out of our enemies.

Nzondo took care of all my needs and expenses when I started working for him. I wasn't the only woman living there with him in Lindelani. He had many girlfriends surrounding him . . . amantombazanyane ancu.[7]

When we served in Nzondo's army, us women were treated just the same as the men. The only difference between us ukuthi thina sasinezinkomo bona babenamatotolozi,[8] but other than that there was no difference in what he expected us to do.

---

[3] I did as I was told

[4] Isidlamlilo translates as 'a person who eats fire'.

[5] provoking people

[6] Inkatha Freedom Party

[7] young girls

[8] we had vaginas and they had testicles

Me and the other women ran a squad known
as Amakhosazane ayisikhombisa . . . the Seven
Sisters. Nzondo sorted us out with police
uniforms and guns.

ZENZILE *rises and removes the lid from the pot.*
Steam rises into the light. She plops the potatoes in.
Musical underscore begins, escalating as the scene
progresses.

ZENZILE: Working for that man I became addicted to the
heat from those fires . . . iphunga lomchamo,[9] paraffin.
The stories people started to tell about me across
this country. Yah, lots of rumours spread about this
Impundulu. [ZENZILE *removes a blanket from the bed*
and drapes it across her shoulders before securing a
black beret on her head. Her shadow stretches across
the back wall, the blanket draped over her shoulders
causing her to resemble a winged bird.] Many said she
used umuthi[10] to turn into that lightning bird that was
setting fire to the people's houses. Others said that
she would bite off the heads of the imfezis,[11] suck the
poison from their throats and then spit it in the eyes
of her enemies when they opened the door to greet
her! Ngiyakutshela![12] [*Beat.*] Why do you think none
of the other women's grandchildren in this hostel

---

[9] the smells of piss
[10] witchcraft
[11] cobras
[12] I'm telling you!

ever come to my room and ask to sit on my lap? Kuze kube inamhlanje ngeke ubone ngane ezocela uswidi kulogogo.[13]

Ey, that Nzondo, he was the one who understood how to use muthi. Yah, that one could even turn into an orange. I'm telling you, an orange . . . the fruit that you eat. [*She retrieves an orange from the sack hanging off the counter and holds it up for Nkulunkulu to inspect.*] We saw it with our own eyes. Sometimes houses would catch fire and all that people would see was an orange rolling down that street and into the bushes. [*She rolls the orange across the stage and watches as it vanishes into the wings.*] But we were all using muthi back then to protect ourselves. That's how I survived this bullet. [*Shows a scar on her hand.*] And this one. [*Gestures to scars on her calf and left buttock.*] Kusanenye esasele esinqeni sami[14] that makes sitting for too long uncomfortable. It's still there!

Lightning begins to flash outside the window. Rain streaks down the pane.

ZENZILE: There in Lindelani, Nzondo taught us how to shoot. They would put up a target and we would practise. [She raises her walking stick to her eye as if

---

[13] No, even to this day, you won't find them coming in here to ask this gogo for sweeties.

[14] And there's one still in my ass

she is aiming a rifle and mimes the action of taking a shot.] If any of the Sisters missed, they would get a beating from one of the big guns of the organisation.

That's why, when he finally gave us the list of those ANC men who murdered my husband, Impundulu knew how to hit her target each and every time.

Music begins to intensify as ZENZILE *retrieves a sjambok[15] from the corner of the room and sets off on a violent rampage, cracking her whip repeatedly against the locker. There is a cracking sound, accompanied by lightning strikes, for each gunshot fired.*

ZENZILE: Nqo[16] . . . Nqo . . . Nqo . . . One strike! . . . Nqo . . . Nqo . . . Two strike! . . . Nqo . . . Nqo . . . Three strike! . . . Nqo . . . Four! . . . Nqo . . . Five! . . . Six! . . . until they were all gone.

The scene changes to a nightmarish flashback. The music builds in intensity and with it arises a cacophony of sounds: sirens, gunfire, shouting, singing, chanting, babies wailing, helicopters passing overhead, buildings catching fire, screams of distress, breaking glass and explosions.

---

[15] The sjambok is a heavy whip traditionally made from hippopotamus or rhinoceros hide, but is also commonly made out of plastic.

[16] Knock (sound of gunshot)

*Smoke fills the room, police searchlights beam
down from the rafters and scan the residence,
ambulance and police siren lights strobe outside
the window.*

Amid the chaos ZENZILE *lurches for the bag of
oranges and begins lobbing them in all directions –
as if they were Molotov cocktails. Oranges flee the
scenes of multiple crimes, rolling in all directions.*
ZENZILE *throws a blanket over her head to hide
from the searchlights falling on the bed, retrieving
her Bible and praying furiously in an attempt to
push the memories away.*

ZENZILE: Eish, we hurt people too much. My life was very
bad. Every night I beg you for forgiveness, I call out
to you and say [*Imploring with tears streaming down
her face.*]: 'Nkulunkulu, with all my heart I'm sorry for
what I did. I was only looking for a place to belong.
I understand why you've punished me like this. I
see now, Nkulunkulu, with the scales having fallen
from my eyes. I see now the person you wanted me
to become. I have put that bird to sleep forever in my
heart, Father. [*As her prayer intensifies, the frenetic
sounds and lightning gradually retreat back into
memory.*] Ngeke ngiphinde ngiyikhiphe.[17] No, I will
never set it free. Ngixolele,[18] Nkulunkulu, ngixolele.

---

[17] I will never let it out again.
[18] Forgive me

Uma kufika isikhathi ngicela ungangivaleli ngaphandle kombuso wakho . . . ungangishiyi baba. Sengishintshile Simakade, ngempela sengishintshile.'[19]

The sound of rain gently falling outside. A silence before ZENZILE *is able to address Nkulunkulu again.*

ZENZILE: You remember, Nkulunkulu, I told you that the Home Affairs said they would phone Nqobile when they had fixed the problem with my death certificate? Remember that girl with the pink nails said they would call us?

Well, Nqobile and I waited and waited. Lutho.[20] Eventually I told my grandchild . . . no, she must take me back – uninvited – to those offices. I must sort this matter out.

---

[19] When the hour arrives don't lock me outside of your kingdom . . . don't leave me here. I've changed, truly I have.

[20] Nothing.

Scene 9

HOME AFFAIRS SHOWDOWN (PART 2)

ZENZILE *grabs her purse and slings it over her shoulder before pushing her wheelchair to centre stage as the lights close in on the scene. As she manoeuvres her chair into position, she insults and curses people she sees in the Home Affairs queue, barging her way to the front, where she plonks herself in the chair and eyes* PINK NAILS *with utter contempt. Once again* ZENZILE *shifts between* PINK NAILS *and herself in the reenactment of the scene.*

PINK NAILS [*chewing gum and rolling her eyes*]: I said we'd phone you! . . .

ZENZILE [*to Nkulunkulu*]: Said Pink Nails. [*To* PINK NAILS.] Why then have I heard nothing from you for over six months?

PINK NAILS: We must deal with many people's struggles in here at once, Gogo. You see our system has confused you with someone else and . . .

ZENZILE: Then make it unconfused. Can't you see that I'm alive? Can't you see I'm in need of my grant money to eat and pay my rent? Ngibuke.[1] Look at me! Look at me with the two good eyes God has given you and tell me ukuthi ngisekhona![2]

PINK NAILS: I can see that but it's not up to me, Gogo.

---

[1] Look.
[2] I'm still here!

ZENZILE: Who is it up to then? Eh? Ngitshele ubani![3]

PINK NAILS: The system.

ZENZILE [*adamant*]: Then teach your system to *see*!

PINK NAILS: It's a machine, Gogo. Ayinamehlo.[4]

ZENZILE [*losing her cool completely*]: What must I do, eh? What must I do to prove to ikhompyutha yakho[5] that I'm still breathing? Give me those scissors on your desk and I will show you that there's still blood moving in these veins! Letha la lesosikere ngizisike khona ngizokupruvela.[6]

PINK NAILS: Lokho akudingekile![7] I'll send another query to the head office and notify you when the matter is resolved.

ZENZILE: Ixazulule manje![8]

PINK NAILS [*a little taken aback*]: There's no need to be rude!

ZENZILE: Rude! Ekse wena![9] . . . You know what's rude? What's rude is that no one even remembered to invite me to my own funeral! [*Beat.*] I'm not leaving this place until your system tells me that I'm living again.

PINK NAILS: There's no need to raise your voice. Vele uphumule![10] Just relax.

---

[3] Tell me who!

[4] It has no eyes.

[5] your computer

[6] Give me those scissors and I will cut myself to prove this to you.

[7] That is not necessary!

[8] Resolve it now!

[9] Hey you!

[10] Just relax, lady!

ZENZILE: Ngiphumule?[11] [*She whacks her walking stick aggressively on the floor.*] ngiRelaxe, heh? What do you mistake me for, eh? . . . A hair straightener? No, I'm not a relaxer . . . I'm not a relaxer at all. Ubongibuza kwabangaziyo ntombazane.[12]

PINK NAILS: But our system . . .

ZENZILE: Do you think I'm scared of your system? Eh? This same system that never once in my life helped me. Never gave me my house when I waited twenty years for it . . . treated me only as a number and never a living, breathing thing. Isystem yakho ngeke ize ingesule kalula kanjalo nje emhlabeni.[13] Never! [*Beat.*] I won't let this government make me stand before a small child like this and beg for my life. [*Beat.*] No, you're too young to know me and you are fortunate for that! Udlala ngomlilo[14] and the next time you see me . . . the next time I'm made to wait in this line ngeke uphinde ungikhohlwe![15]

---

[11] Relax?

[12] You can ask any of my enemies about that.

[13] No, your system cannot wipe me off the face of this earth so easily.

[14] You are playing with fire

[15] you will never forget me!

Scene 10

ZENZILE REBORN

As ZENZILE *wheels her chair back into its corner and returns to sit on her bed, a radio announcement from the 1994 election results plays on the wireless.*

NEWS PRESENTER [*voiceover*]: Now president in all but name, Nelson Mandela swept into the ANC headquarters to address his followers. The outcome had been a virtual certainty all along, but the sense of history was lost on no one. More than merely leading the fight against apartheid, Nelson Mandela came to embody it. The struggle is my life, he said; his personal victory was the victory of an entire nation. Nelson Mandela's inauguration as his country's first democratically elected president is just days away . . .

'Nkosi Sikelel' iAfrika' is being sung triumphantly in the background of the news broadcast. ZENZILE *has had enough. She lurches across the room and switches off the radio.*

ZENZILE: I'll never forget, Nkulunkulu, hearing what was happening with those elections on the radio. The ANC were winning more and more of the people's votes. Yah, that made me go very quiet. [*Beat.*] All of those years of fighting and we were losing . . . we had lost.

A silence.

ZENZILE: You know, when I worked for Nzondo, he told
us that what we were doing for the IFP would make
us all heroes of the struggle. That's what he said.
Angiqambi amanga. Tshela mina sikhona istatue sami
esigcwele amasimba ejuba esimiswe lapha eCity hall
eduze kwesikaQueen? . . . Lutho.[1] [*Chuckling.*] I'm still
waiting. Lutho[2] . . . You won't find an airport or freeway
named after me . . . Maybe a cemetery . . . but that will
be all.

Seventeen years after those first elections, I
walked into Sis Thembi's offices – she was the
ANC councillor at this hostel – and I threw my
IFP membership card in her rubbish bin and told
her I'm leaving this thing called the IFP because
they were making a fool out of me. After all those
elections there was not a single time we were
doing any of the winning. No, I only ever saw
ANC people on the RDP list getting houses and I
now wanted to become a member. But even after
I joined the ANC, Nkulunkulu, I was left waiting
at the bottom of that RDP list thinking my turn
would come. This year it will come . . . maybe the
next one . . . Akukaze kwenzeke.[3]

---

[1] I never lie. But tell me, do you see a statue of me, covered in
pigeon shit, standing beside the queen at the city hall? . . .
Nothing.

[2] Nothing.

[3] It never happened.

The only reason I used to fight for the IFP was because I am bhinca.[4] When we had our meetings, we'd put on our traditional attire and fill up those buses, singing our songs and performing our dances.

She begins to sing a verse of an IFP song.

ZENZILE: uShenge owethu . . . uShenge lo owethu . . . sizobadubula dubula dubula . . . gagagaga.[5]

She makes the sounds of the machine gun and then ululates.

ZENZILE: That was the thing I liked the most about being an IFP member. I didn't even know the differences between the parties.

She now retrieves one of the oranges from the floor and begins peeling it.

ZENZILE: Yah, before you spoke to me, Nkulunkulu, before I learnt your gospel by heart, I was a traditional Zulu woman. Ngangisina ingoma.[6] But that pastor who

---

[4] uneducated

[5] Shenge is ours . . . Shenge is ours . . . we are going to shoot them and shoot them and shoot them. (uShenge refers to the clan name of Prince Mangosuthu Gatsha Buthelezi [27 August 1928 – 9 September 2023], a South African politician and Zulu prince who served as the traditional prime minister to the Zulu royal family from 1954 until his death in 2023. Buthelezi founded the Inkatha Freedom Party [IFP] in 1975.)

[6] I danced traditional dances.

visited me here, he told me it was your wish for me to move away from all this dancing. He said doing that traditional dance would only send me backwards to my old ways . . . my old life . . . impilo engangizama ukuphuma kuyona.[7]

All of that has passed now. You can't change what is behind. And Nzondo? Yah, even that muthi he was taking stopped working. [*She tears a segment off the peeled orange and pops it in her mouth.*] [*Beat.*] He was shot in the head years later . . . shot by a small boy who killed him in his driveway.

[*Still savouring a mouthful of the delicious fruit.*] You know what I miss about having a home of my own, Nkulunkulu? I miss working the land and eating fresh food. Awukwazi nokutshala la,[8] you can't plant on the concrete, kumele isandla singene ephakatheni ukuze uphile.[9] At home I can plant my vegetables and feed myself, all I need is oil and mealie meal. [*Beat.*] That is all I need. Nkulunkulu, you sent me the gifts to make things grow. [*She rises and retrieves her potted tree sapling from the windowsill and puts it proudly beside her.*] See how I've nursed this one from a small seed into a bush.

---

[7] the life I was trying to wash away
[8] You can't plant it here
[9] you have to put your hand in your pocket, so you can live

My gogo gave me this seed from the fruit of her isihlahla samahlala[10] tree. She had one of these there in her garden in Ipharadesi. She said I must take with me a piece of that land wherever I go in life. When my house is finished, I will plant this one outside by the front door. Yah, I have a secret recipe that my gogo taught me to put in the soil to make our vegetables grow. You want to know it, Nkulunkulu? [*Mischievously shaking her head.*] It's a secret kept by us Maseko women. No share . . . no share.

She puts the plant on the ground and reaches for her Bible.

ZENZILE: When I first came to this hostel in 1990, I went to the night school to learn how to read and write, but the only book I've ever read is the one written by you, Nkulunkulu. Ngifundiswe uJehova mina.[11] He is the one who taught me how to read this book from A right up until Z.

It was Pastor Mazibuko from the Return to God gospel church who first came to find me here. He said he had been sent by you to give me a message.

When Mazibuko saw me in this chair . . . he fell to his knees and preached to me about that man

---

[10] monkey apple
[11] Jehovah, that man has been my only teacher.

45

named uJob. He told me my suffering was nothing
compared to that man's. I learnt through him
that my suffering was because I'd done wrong
in your eyes. The moment I let that creature
into my heart, I disrespected your creation.
Ngalesasikhathi ngisawubhodlumlilo[12] I used to
think I was more powerful than you. Can you
believe it, Nkulunkulu! Yah, I used to think that
I could give and take life as easily as changing a
TV channel, but no one but you should ever be in
charge of that remote control.

After the pastor's visit, I decided I would never
touch umuthi[13] again. I took that muthi and
asked a child from this hostel to take it down to
the beachfront and throw it into the sea. Yah,
I wanted to test you, Nkulunkulu, I wanted to
see if you really were the God everyone said you
were. Ngabe kukhona okushintshile?[14] Ai, you
should see my situation now compared to last
year.

ZENZILE *begins to unpeg clothing items from
the line and toss them into the washing basket.
She then sits on the edge of the bed and begins
folding each item as neatly as she can within the
limitations of her one useless hand.*

---

[12] Back when I was eating fire
[13] traditional medicine
[14] Did anything change?

ZENZILE: Yah, when this stroke happened, the doctors
told Thuthukile she must take me back home to die
there. Yah, I was dying . . . I'm serious . . . I was like
a dead body . . . a sack of potatoes. I was just a thing
that had saliva dripping down her chin. Ngizichamele
ngizikakele ngingasenamabrekie.[15] I couldn't stand up
and do this. [*She rises, dancing a little clumsily on the
spot.*] Or this. [*Walks forward painfully.*] Day by day
I feel myself getting stronger. I'm able to stand on my
own now. When this healing began, ohhhhh, I gave
praises to you. Yah, Nkulunkulu, I thank you even now
that I have done my washing and soaked it and hung it
over there. That is something I could never have done
a year ago.

Even before I met you, Nkulunkulu, I knew in my
heart what I was doing for Nzondo was wrong.
I decided to put that old life behind me. My
auntie's husband found a place there for me in
Inanda where I could start my own tuck shop. I
was only interested in izidakwa ezinonile[16] who
sat there the whole day drinking all my beer and
eating my vetkoeks.[17] [*Chuckling.*] My tuck shop
was too popular with those ones.

---

[15] I would shit and urinate on myself and couldn't hold myself.

[16] fat drunks

[17] Vetkoek (fat cake) is a traditional South African fried dough that
is crispy outside, fluffy inside, and often stuffed with sweet or
savoury filling.

ZENZILE *now pulls a green dress with long sleeves from the laundry basket. She holds it up and inspects it.*

Scene 11

THE FALL OF IMPUNDULU

In this scene ZENZILE *speaks the lines of the ANC men, of her grandmother and of the man who rescues her.*

ZENZILE: One Monday, I arrived back at my shop in Inanda from doing a ceremony for my gogo in Ipharadesi. When I arrived there those men were already waiting inside.

Music builds.

ZENZILE: 'Yah, Mpundulu,' they said. 'We've been looking for you.'

I just kept quiet. I didn't say yes or no to any of the questions they asked. Even when they began hitting and kicking me and pushed me into one of their cars.

I kept quiet for most of that drive – I just looked at them until the one man slapped me hard and said, 'Ubukani?[1] . . . Eh? . . . Ubukani klova?'[2]

They asked how many ANC people I had killed and eventually I replied, 'Woooo, there are not

---

[1] What are you looking at?
[2] Klova is an insulting name given to IFP supporters.

49

enough fingers and toes on my hands and feet to count for you.'

'Bangaki?'[3] they asked again, and I answered, 'As many as you yourselves had killed of our IFP members.'

One of the younger ones hit me again and told me to stop being cheeky. Angiqambi amanga.[4] I repeated that we'd all been in the same business, whichever side you were on, we were all as guilty as each other.

That car drove through Amaoti . . . Amaotana, heading to the cemetery eTafuleni.[5] The graveyard there is at the top of a hill and surrounded by bush and umhosha[6] . . . In that bush you will find the bodies of our comrades.

Then they pushed me out of the car and into those bushes. [*She discards the green dress on the floor in front of her.*] There were others already waiting there. I got a hot slap as well as a kick and then another. [*She begins to puppeteer the dress so that the flimsy fabric becomes a rag-doll representation of herself.*] I fell down and stood up.

---

[3] How many?

[4] I never lie.

[5] It is said that in the 1980s when you were taken to eTafuleni Cemetery in Inanda, you knew you would not return alive.

[6] a small stream

Ngiyakhumbula ngizizwa nginokubonga ukuthi kungcono ngoba ngisanda kwenza umsebenzi kagogo, amadlozi ami asasuthi inyama.[7]

I fell down and stood up again. [*The dress rises and falls.*]

As they hit me, I started preparing my way . . . started speaking with okhokho bami[8] . . . Ngezwa sebengibiza.[9] Ngaqala ngakhuluma nokhokho bami . . . ngezwa sebengibiza.[10]

They hit me until there was no place left on my body that was not bleeding. They hit me until I began to see the faces of my parents.

When the time came, one of the councillors held a gun to my head [*She mimes the action, pointing fingers at the dress crumpled in a lifeless heap at her feet.*] and said, 'Linda, how do we know this is the right one? How do we know this is her for sure?'

The men pulled me to my knees and tore my shirt off. [*She takes the dress by the scruff of the neckline and pulls it to her knees and then tears it to one*

---

[7] I remember feeling thankful that I had just held that ritual at my gogo's home and that my ancestors were still satisfied with that meat.

[8] my ancestors

[9] I heard them calling me.

[10] I started speaking with my ancestors . . . and I heard them calling me.

side, shifting the position of her body on the bed.
The room lights dim slightly, and as in Scene 6, a
lightning scar is revealed projected across her back.]

I remembered Gogo tracing the pattern on my
back with her cloth . . .

VOICE OF MEN: Buka![11] . . . Look!

ZENZILE: Gogo telling me my scar looked like a river
growing stronger and stronger.

VOICE OF MEN: It's her!

ZENZILE: Isihlahla sempilo,[12] she had called it.

VOICE OF GRANDMOTHER: The tree of all life.

VOICE OF MEN: The wings of Impundulu!

ZENZILE: 'Linda . . . Linda,' said another voice. 'They say you
can't kill this idemoni[13] with a bullet. Many have tried
but she just comes back stronger than before. [*Beat.*]
Fire . . . fire is the only way to destroy this thing.'

The scar disappears as she turns back to face the
audience.

ZENZILE: There was laughter before I heard them opening
the car boot . . . footsteps . . . petrol burning my eyes as
it spilled over me.

Then they called another man to finish the job.
A man who had been sitting that whole time in

---

[11] Look!
[12] The tree of life
[13] demon

his car. His shadow fell over me. A matchstick
scraped against the box. [*She lights a match.*]

VOICE OF MEN: 'Layitha!'[14] shouted his friends. 'Mshise
mfowethu!'[15]

ZENZILE: The man standing over me said, 'Isikhathi
sesihambile,'[16] feeling for a pulse on my neck before
blowing out his match. 'She's dead already . . . Let's just
leave her here to rot in the bush.'

The cars drove off. I tried to stand, but my legs
no longer felt like they were a part of my body.
Njengonodoli wengane wendwangu olahlwe
phezu kwentaba kadoti.[17]

Again ZENZILE *manipulates the dress to rise
and fall.*

ZENZILE: Hours passed before I heard the wheels of another
car on the dirt.

I felt arms lifting me and laying me in the back
seat of that car . . . hands covering me with a
blanket.

*She rises now and scoops the outfit tenderly into her
arms, laying it on the bed. She sits at the top of the
bed so that the dress's non-existent head appears to*

---

[14] Do it!

[15] Burn her, brother!

[16] It's too late

[17] I lay there like a child's dirty cloth doll left on a rubbish heap.

*be resting on her lap. One of the sleeves hangs to the
side like a lifeless arm.*

ZENZILE: Lying there all I could hear was the driver
whispering something that sounded like 'Ngiyaxolisa'.[18]
His car stopped for a few minutes . . . voices arguing
. . . then we were driving again . . . city lights rushing
across the windows.

VOICE OF RESCUER: Ngiyaxolisa . . . ngiyaxolisa.

ZENZILE: The door opened. Arms laid me on the pavement
outside the Durban station.

She lays the dress on the floor, carefully arranging it.

VOICE OF RESCUER: Ngiyaxolisa.

ZENZILE: For a moment I could see his face in the changing
traffic light . . . green, then red. He was older . . .
thinner . . . with two gold teeth shining at the front.

If I had any air left in my lungs, I would have called
after him . . . named him . . . but his car drove off
and now two policemen were tapping my corpse
with their boots and discussing if I was dead or alive.

They called for an ambulance on their radios, and
while we waited that pavement began to feel like a
pillow under my head.

I shut my eyes and went to sleep for a very long time.

Music climaxes.

---

[18] I'm sorry

Scene 12

RESURRECTION

In this scene ZENZILE, *in her hostel room, speaks as herself to Nkulunkulu. She also speaks the parts of the* PASTOR, MUSA *and members of the congregation. In effect she tells two parallel stories, voicing all the characters in them. When she speaks as herself,* ZENZILE *shifts her body to a different angle and is picked up by a sidelight, which helps differentiate her from the* PASTOR *in the church settings. Throughout this scene, the transitions between the two parallel stories and characters are demarcated by a change in lighting combined with a subtle change of the actor's body positioning.*

ZENZILE: I woke up in the hospital seven months later. Yah, for seven months, Nkulunkulu, I'd slept without dreaming. Angiqambi amanga.[1] And only in the seventh month did I open my eyes and find the strength to ask myself where or who I was. Back then my body was still being held together by plaster.

My family members kept on visiting me, right until the end of the year, right up until I left that hospital. Later I heard that many people in KwaMashu and Ipharadesi had been celebrating the death of Impundulu. [*Beat.*] There were big parties. [*She shakes her head while folding the*

---

[1] I never lie.

green dress neatly and depositing it back in the laundry basket.] I feel very sorry that they didn't believe those who had warned them that it's impossible to kill me.

You know, Nkulunkulu, Pastor Mazibuko used to visit my room at the hostel every weekend to pray for me after my stroke, and when he saw those miracles you were working on me he said [*She speaks in voice of* PASTOR.]: 'It's time, Sis Zenzile, for you to be born again at the church . . . It's time for our congregation to lay their hands on you and pray.'

When I told this to my neighbour Ma Thwala, wooooh weeee, she was very excited for me. She already attended this church and said that I must go with her on Sunday. But I laughed. How could I put foot in God's temple looking like a person who sells things down there by the taxi rank at Warwick Junction?[2] Ma Thwala gave me a set of smart clothes and a headscarf. [*She retrieves a formal black shawl and doek from the washing line and begins to dress for church.*] She told me to be dressed and ready on Sunday morning to go with her. [*Beat.*] I woke up very early to prepare myself.

---

[2] Warwick Junction, also known as Warwick Triangle, is a transportation and trading hub in the city of Durban.

After I was discharged from that hospital, I returned to Lindelani to prove to my Sisters and comrades that I was still alive. Me and my Sisters then visited Nzondo to collect our guns and uniforms before he handed me the names and addresses of the comrades who had taken me there to eTafuleni Cemetery over a year ago.

Kwaba njengoba ngikutshela nje.[3] Angiqambi amanga![4] I never used to send people alone to do my business for me. No, I always cleaned up after myself. Back then I had not been taught by Jehovah to turn the other cheek. [*She begins tying the black head scarf ceremoniously around her head.*] There was much I still needed to learn. [*Beat.*] Back then all I knew was that when you made the mistake of harming Impundulu, she would hunt you and find you and harm you very badly in return.

A rumble of thunder.

ZENZILE *pushes the wheelchair downstage and takes her place behind it as if she were a pastor standing at the pulpit addressing his congregation.*

ZENZILE [*to Nkulunkulu*]: When Ma Thwala and I arrived at the Return to God gospel church, Pastor Mazibuko was giving a sermon from your Book of Revelation.

---

[3] It was exactly as I'm telling you.
[4] I never lie!

Lighting change as ZENZILE *assumes the voice and gesticulations of the* PASTOR.

PASTOR [*in full evangelical flight*]: Look around, brothers and sisters. Siyeza isikhathi sokwahlulelwa![5]

ZENZILE [*aside*]: Yoh, that pastor knew his gospels! I sat there shocked by the things he was telling us. Wooooh weeee, he went on and on about . . .

PASTOR: John and his judgements . . . the four galloping horsemen . . . the breaking of the seals and the blowing of the trumpets. Those earthquakes ezozamazamisa abantu emhlabeni njengenja inikina amazenze ayilumayo,[6] and that star, brothers and sisters, that star – as big as a mountain – that will fall from the sky and poison the rivers and land so we may never eat or drink from them again.

Lighting change.

Dressed in her black shawl and headscarf, ZENZILE *resembles a cloaked bird . . . an angel of death . . . Impundulu.*

ZENZILE: The heat was very bad on the evening my Sisters and I set out to complete our final job. Flying ants were swarming under the street lights.

---

[5] The hour of judgement is approaching!

[6] shake the people from the surface of the earth like fleas from an itchy dog's back

Coming over the hill there by Phoenix, I could see clouds building up over the sea. Spider webs of electricity spreading across the sky. And my head . . . hot . . . hot . . . hot . . . Ligxabha njengeketela ekade libila elinganakwe muntu.[7]

Lighting change.

The storm is building as backdrop to the next two scenes, with more frequent flashes of lightning.

ZENZILE: Pastor Mazibuko went on about . . .

PASTOR: The bowls of fire which the seven angels will empty on our heads from heaven. The flames mixed with blood that would eat up all the grass and trees. The giant imfezis[8] that will slither over the ruins of the world and devour all those who do not bear the seal of God on their foreheads . . . those not yet baptised by the blood of Christ.

Lighting change.

ZENZILE: That night Impundulu and Amakhosazane ayisikhombisa[9] swept down with the winds and rains. Nqo . . . Nqo . . . Nqo . . . one strike! [*Lightning crash.*] Nqo . . . Nqo . . . two strikes! [*Lightning crash.*] Nqo . . . Nqo . . . three strikes! [*Lightning crash.*] Nqo . . . four! [*Lightning crash.*] Nqo . . . five! . . .

---

[7] Hot like a kettle left on a stove long after its whistling.

[8] cobras

[9] the Seven Sisters

ZENZILE *picks up her sjambok and stalks about*
the room whipping the locker repeatedly with
violent precision and focus. Lightning strikes and
strobes wildly as the shots ring out for this brief
but terrifying interlude. Eventually she regains
composure and steps back into the light, a little out
of breath.

ZENZILE: . . . until they were gone.

Me and my Sisters worked till the early
hours until there was only one name left on
our list.

When I saw it, I told my Sisters that we were
done for the night. We would leave this man for
another time.

Lighting change.

PASTOR [*manic*]: The foolishness, my brothers and sisters,
of throwing away the keys to Christ's kingdom when
they have been handed to you. When Jehovah is
reaching out his hand . . . he's reaching out his hand.
Phendukani[10] . . . Phendukani, my brothers and
sisters . . . reach out and take his hand. Phendukani
. . . Phendukani, bazalwane . . . phakamisani izandla
zenu nizinikele kuye[11] . . . No, there shall be no
mourning . . . nor crying . . . nor pain . . . Your old life

---

[10] Repent
[11] Repent, brethren . . . raise your hands and surrender to him.

has passed away[12] . . . Idlulile[13] . . . Idlulile, brother and sisters.

Lighting change.

ZENZILE: I arrived outside Musa's house three weeks later. His wife showed me in. That man and his two daughters were seated around the table, preparing to eat a meal. They asked if I would like to join them.

When the girl asked how I knew her father, I explained to her that as children we had been best friends . . . we used to swim together in the river by our parents' house.

That man then asked if he could pray and we joined hands while he blessed the meal. It was only when he tried to cut the chicken that I could see how badly his hands were trembling.

After the meal, I told him I needed to fetch something for him from my car. While we walked together, he begged that nothing happen in front of his family. I agreed that we would complete our business outside . . . ngasese.[14]

---

[12] A reference to Revelation 21:4: 'He will wipe every tear from their eyes. There will be no more death or mourning or crying or pain, for the old order of things has passed away.'

[13] It's passed away.

[14] in private

While we walked he told me that all those men who harmed me were gone. 'Bafile,[15] Sis Zenzile!' he said. 'Bafile.'

Then I went round [*She crosses behind the wheelchair.*] and opened the boot of my car as he shut his eyes and began praying again.

'Vula amehlo,'[16] I said. 'Vula!'

A strain of music. ZENZILE's *hands are concealed under the black shawl she wears. She holds the moment, enjoying the power until finally revealing two open hands . . . an offering.*

ZENZILE: I filled his arms with two blankets, a week of groceries and a stuffed toy for each of his daughters and I thanked him.

He knelt at my feet, hitting his fist against his chest.

MUSA: Ngixolele,[17] Sis Zenzile . . . As long as I live, I will never find peace knowing the suffering I caused you and your family. Ngixolele.

ZENZILE: 'That is behind us, Musa Bophela . . . Idlulile,'[18] I replied, getting back into my car and reversing out of his driveway.

---

[15] Dead

[16] Open your eyes

[17] Forgive me

[18] It's passed away

ZENZILE *shrinks into the wheelchair and, using her feet, pushes herself slowly backwards into the darkness.*

Lighting change.

ZENZILE *rises out of the chair with hands raised and steps into a celestial beam of light that meets her from the rafters of the theatre.*

PASTOR: Come, Sister Zenzile. [*Calling her to the front of the church.*] The moment has arrived for you to accept Jesus into your heart. Let us put our hands upon you and pray.

ZENZILE *sits back in the chair and slowly wheels herself forward.*

ZENZILE: Ma Thwala released the brake on my chair and began to wheel me to the front. As we moved down the aisle all that noise and singing and excitement began to fade away.

Pew by pew people began to walk out the door. [*Beat.*] I'm telling you. Angiqambi amanga.[19]

Then a bald man from the back yelled . . . [*She rises, bellowing.*]

MAN: That woman will curse this church just by coming in here! That idemoni[20] used to eat fire. She murdered

---

[19] I never lie.
[20] demon

our families and set fire to our homes. Akayifanele
imithandazo yethu.[21] Ngeke![22]

ZENZILE: Then a gogo yelled on her way out . . . [*She waves
her walking stick accusingly.*]

GOGO: There will never be a place for Impundulu in the
New Jerusalem. She will be turned away at the gates of
Christ's kingdom. I will make sure to get there before
her and when I do . . . I will padlock those gates behind
me. [*Beat.*] May she never know the grace of our
merciful God . . . May she never find peace in this life
or the next one. Amen.

*Music climaxes and the lights fade, restoring the
hostel room setting.*

---

[21] She doesn't deserve our prayers.

[22] Never!

Scene 13

THE CLEANSING

ZENZILE: Day by day, Nkulunkulu, you are helping me . . .
helping me to wash away all that dirtiness. A woman
who once lived the life of a man . . . You are cleansing me.
[*Beat.*] When I see a person feeling sorry for me, I say
no, no, no, that's not how my God wants it. I, the person
who had this stroke, am not feeling sorry for myself, so
why now must you? It's not your business to feel sorry
for me. No, I don't want anyone to pity me. Ngenzeni ke
mina ngalokudatshukelwa? Ngeke ngikuphuze, ngeke
ngikudle, ngeke ngikubheme, ngeke ngikwazi ngisho
ukukudayisa . . . inonsense nje yento engenamsebenzi.[1]

ZENZILE *begins her bathing ritual. She lugs a bucket
of hot water from the stove and pours it into a plastic
tub at the foot of her bed. She removes a dressing
gown from the washing line and lays it beside her. As
she removes the gown she notices a frilly bra hanging
on the line and inspects it suspiciously.*

ZENZILE: Yah, Nqobile, my granddaughter, she has been
hiding from me for many days now. Is it because I
embarrass her with my rudeness? [*Beat.*] I'm telling
you, it's her behaviour she needs to be embarrassed by,
Nkulunkulu. Yah, all those different men . . . And what

---

[1] What must I do with this pity, eh? I can't drink it or eat, smoke or
even sell it . . . no, it's a useless thing, this pity-pity.

must happen? . . . The next time she visits it will be to tell me she has HIV, just like her mother.

ZENZILE *undresses down to her petticoat. She sits on the edge of the bed and dunks her cloth into the tub of water, wringing it out.*

ZENZILE: Wooooh weeee, I've seen too many women cursed by this thing in the past. Yah, Nkulunkulu, I feel that pain when a person gets sick and the world turns away from them. Kubuhlungu kimina ukubona lokho.[2] I told you that my daughter Thuthukile has it. When I first learnt she was suffering from this thing, my aunty had died two months before, so I knew what it was. It wasn't like it is today, where someone can live a normal life . . . Back then it was very different.

The women in our family said we mustn't bring the body of my aunty into the house. When I arrived, I saw she was being kept outside and I asked the women if they had bathed her and they said they hadn't. When I asked why, they whispered it was because she had caught this thing. [*She holds up three fingers to symbolise HIV and speaks as if she is one of the women.*] 'Hayibo, Zenzile, it's too dangerous to touch her! You'll catch it if you try.'

---

[2] That is very painful for me to see.

'Umbhedo,'[3] I said, wheeling that coffin
into that house. I asked everyone to leave
[*Sarcastically.*] in case the HIV would fly from
that dead body and stick to them. [*Chuckling.*]
After I said that, they all left that room in a
hurry.

As she speaks she begins washing her own body,
slowly and meticulously.

ZENZILE: I slanted her coffin to one side and I let the
body roll out. I cut her out of the plastic sheet and
held her with my thighs, washing, washing her
entire body.

She washes her arms, armpits and neck before
wringing out the cloth in the tub.

ZENZILE: Then I dressed her in her nicest clothes, and
combed her hair before wrapping a scarf around her
head. I prepared that coffin like I was making a bed,
laying down a blanket and a pillow so she would sleep
peacefully.

As she washes her legs, she leans forward.

ZENZILE: Then I whispered in her ear and I promised her,
promised that I would make sure she would be given a
proper burial.

---

[3] Nonsense

'Ngeke kube khona hlazo,[4] aunty, no more shame will visit the women in our family.'

She slides the tub of water under the bed and begins to dry herself off with a small towel.

---

[4] There will be no more shame

Scene 14

BURIAL PRAYER

ZENZILE: Yah, I'm telling you, Nkulunkulu, I've seen more plagues, floods and diseases here in KwaZulu than even Moses did during his time on this earth. Angiqambi amanga.[1] [*Beat.*] Even this Covid, what-what . . . There were many older people dying around me in this hostel. I got sick with it too. My results were positive, but it was only for a few days before I was better again. Yah, even Covid version 2019, version 2020 . . . 21 . . . 22 visited my body and then decided it was not safe for it to live in there . . . It packed its bags to move in with the next-door neighbour instead. [*Chuckling.*] Even that thing was scared of me. Ngiyakuchazela![2]

She applies Vaseline to her arms and legs before covering herself in the dressing gown.

ZENZILE: I'm still here after all these things. Ma Twala says, 'Ay, Sis Zenzile, you are not made like the rest of us. You will live past the Judgement Day. Uma sekuphele konke uyosala wedwa la.'[3]

The other day I even asked one of Dudu's boys, Sizwe, while he was helping lay those bricks for

---

[1] I never lie.
[2] I'm telling you!
[3] When everything is gone you will be the only one left here.

me there in Ipharadesi, to also dig my grave for me. Angisenawo amandla okuyimbela umgodi ojule ngaleyondlela.[4] I asked Sizwe to dig it there next to my new house beside the graves of my ancestors. Ngamtshela ukuthi akomba umgodi oshona phansi ngempela ngoba ngiwumuntu onenkani . . . ngiyoba nayo ngisho sengifile.[5]

I've given my child instructions that – if she does not go before me – then she must pack that soil very tightly and pour concrete on the top so not even the summer rains can release me. No, they must make sure that once they put me inside . . . that is that . . . I never return to life again. Yah, kuyofanele benze isiqiniseko sokuthi bangilalisa ngibheke phansi ebhokisini ukuze ngingabuyi nje ngizoba idlozi elibi.[6]

Yah, it's a sad situation there by my home after the floods. [*Looking out of the window.*] All that stands on the top of that hill are the foundations, a doorway without a door and a big empty hole beside it. My daughter says that I'll be sleeping in that grave long before I ever get to sleep in a

---

[4] I don't have the strength to dig holes that deep for myself anymore.

[5] I told him to dig that hole very, very deep because I'm a stubborn one . . . even in death.

[6] This sentence relates to a certain burial procedure in which someone is buried face down so they can never return and become troublesome ancestors.

bed in that house, and maybe she's right. Maybe, Nkulunkulu, if you are finally ready to release me, she will be proven right. I'm ready now, Nkulunkulu. [*Beat.*] Ngikhathele manje.[7]

You know, it will probably be those people from the Home Affairs who will put me in that ground for good. Yah, still no SASSA grant . . . no ID . . . no telephone calls. [*Beat.*] It's been two years of this nonsense, and so early this morning I decided I would pay them a final visit.

---

[7] I'm tired now.

Scene 15

ZENZILE'S REVELATIONS! HOME AFFAIRS SHOWDOWN (PART 3)

A rumble of thunder as the storm circles back for its final crescendo. ZENZILE *means business. She grabs her purse and a black umbrella and pushes the wheelchair angrily into position, cursing in isiZulu as she goes. Lights shrink around the scene as she takes her seat for a final showdown with* PINK NAILS.

ZENZILE: I waited for over eight hours in that queue before pink fingernails looked up from behind her computer. [*Speaking to* PINK NAILS.] Yah, uphelile u two years manje.[1] Two years of you telling me the same thing, and today what's your story, child?'

PINK NAILS [*pretending not to recognise her*]: Igama lakho?[2]

ZENZILE: Don't play games with me. [*She strikes the desk with her umbrella.*] You know my name. Wazi kahle ukuthi ngizokwenzani la.[3]

PINK NAILS: I'm afraid I'm going to have to ask . . .

ZENZILE: Let me speak to your manager.

PINK NAILS: He's not here today, Gogo.

ZENZILE: Then let me speak to that man there in that picture behind your desk. [*Pointing with her umbrella.*] Get

---

[1] it's been two years now

[2] Your name?

[3] You know exactly what I'm here for.

that man on the telephone and tell him I wish to speak with him.

PINK NAILS: That's not possible.

ZENZILE: Ngobani?[4]

PINK NAILS: That man is the president of South Africa.

ZENZILE: And what is his problem? Does he think he is too important to take my calls . . . to care about my little life? Does he not remember how much of my own life I sacrificed so that he can sit there and smile like that when he gets his picture taken? Does he not yet know that it's us . . . us . . . the gogos of this nation who hold it together when others are just prepared to sit back and let it fall apart. [*Beat.*] No, I will teach that man to care.

PINK NAILS: I'm going to need your full name and ID number to process your query, Mrs . . .

ZENZILE: Zenzile Maseko.

PINK NAILS: Spell that for me?

ZENZILE *is about to spell out her name but pauses for a moment. There is a rumble of thunder and flash of lightning. She spells out each letter forcefully.*

ZENZILE: *I . . . M . . . P . . . U . . . N . . . D . . . U . . . L . . .U.*

PINK NAILS: Excuse?

ZENZILE: Ungizwile ntombazane.[5]

---

[4] Why not?
[5] You heard me, girl.

73

PINK NAILS [*confused*]: iIpu . . . ini?[6]

ZENZILE: Im-pun-dulu! Type that in . . . Type it! . . . If you're
still going to tell me that Zenzile Maseko died eleven
years ago in uMzimkhulu, usimoshelani isikhathi
sami?[7] . . . Maybe Impundulu is the name that system
will recognise. Type it in now and see . . . ubuke[8] how
your machine's keys qhaqhazela[9] when it remembers
who I am. [*Firmly.*] Type it!

The lights in the office flicker and trip, leaving
ZENZILE *underlit by a floor light that enhances the*
menace and determination on her face.

PINK NAILS: I'm afraid, Gogo, our system has gone offline
now with the load shedding. You are going to have to
wait now till the power comes back on.

ZENZILE: No! Ngeke ukwazi ukungibulala mina![10] You
cannot kill me. Each time I pull myself out of those
holes, dust myself off and carry on. I carry on and on
and on and on because that is what this life has cursed
me to do. Yah, they've shot, cut, stabbed and beaten
me, broken every bone in this body, hung tyres around
my neck, poured petrol and pissed on my corpse.
They've spilled alcohol in my ancestors' names . . . sat
vigils through the nights . . . sung funeral songs over

---

[6] what?
[7] then why waste my time?
[8] look
[9] tremble
[10] You can't kill me!

and over again, and now what must happen, eh? You want me to believe your president's computer has killed me where none of these other things could? [*Laughs heartily.*]

PINK NAILS [*glancing around, frightened*]: I'm going to call the security now, Gogo!

ZENZILE: No, do not provoke me, child, for when this creature comes again none of you will have an office left to return to in the morning. Yah, all of these things you see here . . . zinkomishi zekhofi nama teaspoons[11] . . . names and surnames . . . walls . . . computers . . . framed pictures of fat ministers . . . dates of birth . . . dates of death . . . numbers and certificates . . . all of it will be gone before the sun rises. Angiqambi amanga.[12]

No, you cannot kill me. I've been here before you and will be here long, long after . . . Long after you and your family and children's children are forgotten. Yah, here after those politicians and their supporters and their enemies and their computers and their systems have erased and eaten each other.

Tremors from the lightning shake the windowpanes of the building. The wind begins to howl outside.

---

[11] these coffee cups and teaspoons
[12] I never lie.

ZENZILE: Never again, uyangizwa?[13] . . . Never again made
to serve as another's umthakathi[14] . . . weapon . . .
comrade . . . isibunu[15] . . . isifebe[16] or whore. What a
world I will be left with soon, eh? Free, child . . . free
for evermore.

No, no man left to stand as my leader . . . lord
. . . god . . . king . . . commander . . . president . . .
deceiver!

No one's soldier, follower, servant or wife. With
Jehovah's book as my pulpit, I'll rise up – with
venom in my veins and lightning on my tongue – to
preach from the revelations written by my own life!

Lightning strikes. ZENZILE'S *tone shifts to that
of a preacher mid-sermon. She rises from her
wheelchair and pushes it to one side, claiming all of
the playing space.*

ZENZILE: Lutho awusoze wangibulala mina.[17] I'll be here
past John's judgements. Past the coming of the
horseman, the breaking of the seals, the sounding of
the trumpets and the pouring of the bowls. Past the
earthquakes, pestilences, storms, the clouds of ash that
suffocate the sun and moon, the floods and swarms.

---

[13] you hear me?

[14] witch

[15] vagina

[16] slut

[17] No, you cannot kill me.

Past the melting of the ice, drying of the rivers and dying of the land. After those plagues have sucked the final breaths from the remaining sinners' lips and I've washed and sung the last corpse left to sleep there deep . . . deep . . . deep in the ground.

Another crash. Music building.

ZENZILE: Past the reckoning, the reaping, the Second Coming! Past Jehovah returning to guide his flocks into heaven's pastures and padlocking the pearly gate behind him. [*Beat.*] I'll still be here!

No more lists or lines, no more suffering or shame. With hands raised to their heavens, I'll reclaim the dance of my ancestors . . . stamp out the coals left by hell's eternal flames.

She begins a traditional Zulu dance now, chanting defiantly. She clutches her umbrella in one fist and punches at the sky. She raises a leg uncomfortably before stamping it forcefully back to the earth. She covers the floor space of her tiny room as she carries out this ritual, wincing in pain with each determined stomp. The music ends . . . Her body slows . . . recalls its age . . . brokenness . . . its earthly limitations.

At the end of the dance, rain begins to fall, streaking down the windowpane and its sound filling the theatre. ZENZILE *cranes her head back to meet it. Extending both arms, she lets go of the umbrella, surrendering to the sensations. She turns a slow circle before confronting* PINK NAILS *and the audience for a final time.*

ZENZILE: And when those first rains fall again to cool the steaming earth and there's nothing . . . not a soul or human left. Even after that . . . I . . . Zenzile Maseko . . . life giver . . . life taker . . . Isidlamlilo[18] . . . Impundulu will remain.

---

[18] Fire Eater

Scene 16

PEACE

The storm calms. The torrential downpour subsides into a soft, soothing patter. ZENZILE *stands centre stage, peering out – out beyond* PINK NAILS *and the Home Affairs office, beyond the audience, the theatre.*

ZENZILE: Yah, you will find her there. There at the top of that hill, sitting there laying the final bricks to her house, sitting there on that cursed patch of earth, with the dying stars above and the stinking river below.

And if, Nkulunkulu, you see that she is lonely and you take pity on her, she will offer you one of her ribs – but on one condition . . . that you send her another woman hayi indoda nje engenamsebenzi.[1]

ZENZILE *slides off her dressing gown and receives it again into her open arms. It's as if her request for a female companion has been granted and she hugs the garment close, breathing in its scent.*

ZENZILE: Then, when that soil is ready, she will plant her gogo's tree back in the earth. [*She cradles the monkey apple sapling in her arms before kneeling to place it on the ground centre stage.*] She will mix up that special

---

[1] and not some useless man

recipe, caring for that young tree until it bears the first fruits so that life may begin again . . . life may return.

She makes a final offering to Nkulunkulu and the audience by sliding the sapling into the last remaining sliver of light. She then sits on the corner of her bed and smiles serenely.

ZENZILE: Yah, at last silence will have descended over the hills and valleys and she will be at peace . . . peace with the wings of the lightning bird burnt into her back . . . peace with the imfezis[2] and wild dogs of Ipharadesi curled up and snoring on her soft warm lap.

She turns away from the audience, stroking an imaginary serpent. The lightning scar stretches and glows across her back for a final moment, mirrored by the image of the sapling branches centre stage.

The lights fade.

Darkness.

Just the sounds of rain and a lonely distant wind blowing over the ruins of all the earth.

END

---

[2] cobras

Afterword

Q&A WITH NEIL COPPEN AND MPUME MTHOMBENI

Dylan McGarry

In this reflective discussion, the creators of Isidlamlilo/The Fire Eater, *Neil Coppen and Mpume Mthombeni, address questions posed by co-producer and education sociologist Dylan McGarry. Together they delve into the essence of this Empatheatre production, examining the character Zenzile Maseko as a powerful symbol of defiance and care in the face of adversity. Her journey through a political and historical purgatory reconfigures the stereotypical archetype of the stoic black African grandmother, emphasising the complexities of human experience.*

Dylan: This play comes at a time when all South Africans feel like survivors, having endured and still enduring the HIV/AIDS pandemic of the 1990s, the Covid-19 pandemic, rolling blackouts, climate anxiety and an almost endless list of apocalyptic catastrophes. As these horrors fold into each other, we realise we require some ways of staying with the anxiety of them. So to begin, I would love to know from both of you, how has making this play helped you defy death in the face of crises and stay with the full reality of the problems we face?

Neil: KwaZulu-Natal (KZN) is both of our homes, and our work as theatre makers and storytellers has been greatly inspired by this province and its people. But for all its beauty and magic, KZN has always been a land of extremes. There is this underlying sense that things could erupt into chaos at any moment, due either to political instability or to forces such as natural disasters. The writing of *Isidlamlilo/The Fire Eater* was set in motion during the July 2021 riots. We were just coming out of the Covid-19 lockdown when a massive wave of civil unrest swept across the province. For several days we were surrounded by the sounds of gunfire and helicopters hovering overhead. Malls and factories were looted and set alight and toxic plumes of smoke blackened the skies and poisoned the rivers. It was an incredibly dystopian and terrifying moment in time and I remember calling Mpume and saying, 'I don't know what to do with this anxiety. I don't know where to put it.'

Out of our conversations, we resolved to return to a haunting interview from years ago, when we had been working on an oral history project with the Urban Futures Centre. The interview was with a woman staying at the Thokoza Women's Hostel in Durban who had served as an Inkatha Freedom Party (IFP) assassin in the 1980s, when KZN was dragged into a prolonged civil war in the build-up to South Africa's first democratic elections. That woman's story became the basis of the story told by Zenzile Maseko in the play. Something about Zenzile's story helped articulate the current moment we found ourselves in, helped us to grapple with the political messiness, the disappointments, the deceptions and frustrations that had led to a recurrence of this mayhem and violence. All art, I believe, is born from the channelling of a series of questions and anxieties, and I suppose this play became a way for us to mould the raw materials of that moment into something more tangible, which seemed a more constructive activity than stockpiling canned foods and watching the news.

The first scene of the play we wrote was Zenzile's final 'I'm still here' monologue. That speech was written with the sound of helicopters and police sirens wailing outside. The only way I knew how to move through the fear was to let Zenzile be my guide. While most of us imagine the apocalypse as a distant future event, Zenzile had survived it every waking minute of her life. It was in moments such as the one we were facing that she knew exactly what to do.

Dylan: Mpume, you perform Zenzile every night, which means you enter into her world every day. How has this work helped you face the almost impossible crises we witness in South Africa daily?

Mpume: I would say firstly that it's not easy portraying a character like Zenzile, who has done deeds that I have never done, unspeakable things, violent things. It is not easy to enter into the mind of someone who has done such things. It requires great empathy. I had to explore deep within myself to find some similarities or some understanding, even sympathy, and try to find an answer for how this woman could become an assassin. How did she come to be this kind of person? She faced terrifying violence before this, and terrible things happened to her. I had to look at those things with her, and then look at myself in relation to those hardships. What would I have done? I came to realise that no matter how big your hardship is, or how small, if it's hard . . . it's hard. We cannot judge. One person may say, 'Yours is not so hard, I've had it much worse.' But no, if I say this thing is hard for me, then it's hard for me. We must accept and empathise where people are at.

As I was formulating the character of Zenzile with Neil, I was searching, I was spending time with death. It was the height of the Covid-19 pandemic and so many people in my life, and around me, were dying. And then it was the floods, so many losses. Death was a constant companion in those months. So I had to deal with that, and Zenzile helped me to not look away, to stay with it all.

Dylan: Death is certainly something that this play stays close to, but also somehow goes beyond. *Isidlamlilo/The Fire Eater* feels like a contemporary odyssey, in which Zenzile takes us through a political and historical purgatory that is our young democracy. She re-narrates the 'hero's journey' trope with her own undying body. In *Isidlamlilo*, the world is reworked through the body/memory of a Zulu grandmother, who we fall in love with, are repulsed by and empathise with all at once. Zenzile reconfigures the romanticised stereotype of the 'stoic black African grandmother' and reminds us that no innocent position exists. Why was it important for you to reframe this archetype?

Mpume: Your question makes me think of a word or phrase in isiZulu which says the mothers are inzalabantu. They give birth to people. Every human being comes from a woman, and then what happens? Women are shunned and shamed.

She is told she is weak. Eh? A woman is told by men that she has no strength. Yet, before he is a man, that little boy lives in your belly for nine months, he eats what you are eating, he breathes your breath, and then you push him out while experiencing intense pain – and we do all this with love. So many women in this country give birth to people that could hurt them, or hurt other women. We are bringing life into this world, but there is the possibility that what we have birthed can be destructive or destroyed! I think Zenzile shows us that no, we do not accept this violence anymore, that as mothers, as gogos, we are the creators and also the destroyers and we can start this all again, and that, as women, even our destructive elements come from a place of love.

Neil: Mpume, I was reminded of your own journey when we were driving up to Joburg together and listening to that podcast you were featured on for the Nelson Mandela Foundation. In the interview you spoke about confronting patriarchy while growing up. You described the huge resistance you faced from your father, who did everything he could to ensure you would never succeed in building a career for yourself as an artist; how he thought that being an actor was the same as being a sex worker. It struck me how hard you had to fight to secure a place in the world, to claim that space, to become the performer we love and respect today.

Mpume: Telling Zenzile's story, to be able to stand up as a woman and tell a true story, that is so powerful for me. The idea that men can sit there in my audience and listen to me for an hour and forty minutes. This play makes them open their hearts. I get to make a home for myself in their hearts.

Every person who spends time in this show, with me, with my ancestors, comes out with their minds shifted. These are the stories that we need to be told, need to be told over and over again. I'm so grateful I'm part of telling these stories.

Dylan: While the play is very much inspired by real people and events, and is situated in a real time and place, there is this wonderful use of magical realism and myth. I am interested in how you worked carefully to subvert religious texts, parables and archetypes. In a sense you are rewriting and reclaiming many of these texts from an African feminist perspective – a perspective that is absent from the source material.

Neil: You know, I love the moment at the end of the play when Zenzile rewrites the biblical Book of Revelation. In this moment, rather than delivering her sermon by the book, she throws away the biblical text and works to reconcile her pain, her struggle and the ways she has been failed by others by rewriting it with her own life experience. As someone who is intimately familiar with the apocalypse (by virtue of surviving it daily), she reveals what the apocalypse looks like according to her own life.

Mpume: She also sees herself as a sort of Eve figure, or maybe it's Lillith. For this play we delved deep into research around women in mythic history and interwove this with Zulu and biblical mythology. So Ipharadesi stands as this sort of garden that Zenzile is exiled from as a child after she is accused of witchcraft, and at the end, in her narration of the story, she gets to return and reclaim it.

Neil: This is not Eve without agency, as she is mostly depicted; she's an Eve that has been locked out of the gates of Paradise but storms back in at the end and restarts it with her grand-mother's sapling, taming the serpent and shrugging off God's offer of sending her another useless Adam in the process. Given the colonial history of Christianity, we felt it is impor-tant to see an African woman reinvent and articulate these stories on her own terms. I'm a firm believer that the myths and stories on which we base our beliefs about the world and each other fail to meet the contemporary moment, and it's our duty as writers and storytellers to ensure they do.

Mpume: Zenzile's relationship with the snake, and with the tree of life (and wisdom), is important. The way she has been bitten by the imfezi (cobra) and holds the venom of that snake in her veins, the lightning on her tongue. She carries inside her the powers of the elements and creatures that have tried to destroy her. She can start fires and summon the lightning, but she also has the gifts of growing and renewing things. These are cleansing and healing powers.

Dylan: It is very important that you both avoid romanticis-ing 'the African woman'. So many people do. They use words like 'resilient' or 'stoic' to describe this figure. But you both throw out those signifiers and stereotypes and replace them with rich layers and complexities of the experience of African women in relation to a very real apocalypse taking place in South Africa now and in the past. It resonates at the core of what Empatheatre is, a place of radical love. What I love about this play is that it refuses to look away. It stays with the reality of everything. It is a very powerful gesture of love.

I am thinking of the way Zenzile is the only person willing to tend to the body of a person who died of AIDS in the early 1990s. There is a radical kind of transgressive love that plays out there.

Mpume: In relation to that scene, I often think of how everyone has a journey, everyone has a purpose. Are we coming here to teach or to nurture? Whatever we arrive to do, we must learn, in ourselves, to practise radical care, to love, to tend to the world that we are living in. No one just wakes up in the morning and says, 'I'm going to be an assassin, I'm going to be a killer'. No, there are circumstances – unkindness, suffering, poverty, exclusion – that push someone to those terrible decisions. I think Zenzile shows us that we are all capable of doing horrific things if we are pushed to it; she also shows us how we can redeem ourselves from this, and how we can care in more radical ways.

Neil: I think many of the interviews with the women in the Thokoza hostel in Durban underscore this lesson, and they show how we can confront trauma head-on and gaze into its depths. When we do this, a unique form of compassion emerges – a compassion that is born from truly recognising and acknowledging things that aren't always easy or comfortable. Zenzile's love emerges from a profound depth that is shaped by her experiences. Her life, marked by episodes of revenge and rage, brutality and bravery, love and extraordinary loss, holds lessons beyond the ordinary. Many South Africans could share similar narratives, where the ability to continue loving despite hardships is a deeply moving aspect.

Dylan: You refer to the interviews of women who inspired this play. Neil mentioned earlier that one oral history haunted you the most. Tell us why this particular story required further attentive re-storying, re-worlding?

Mpume: It all began with those ten oral histories from the Thokoza Women's Hostel. Among them was a remarkable story about a woman assassin. I must admit, I had never come across the notion of a woman assassin before. That in itself was deeply intriguing for me; I had so many questions. As an actor, I seek out roles that present challenges, challenges for my soul and for others. Characters that demand a level of complexity, that call on different forms of empathy and attentiveness. Those that help you think about questions of what it means to be human in this country and in this world of ours.

Neil: Around ten years ago Mpume and I collaborated on *Tin Bucket Drum*, a one-woman show that offered a more simplistic political allegory of the time. The notion of revisiting the one-woman format together and tackling issues that excited and terrified us at this point in our careers was hugely exciting. There is tremendous potency in a one-woman vehicle in which Mpume holds the reins; she is a master of this sort of storytelling. Those who have seen her in action will know exactly what I'm talking about.

Dylan: Don't you think a lot of the work we do as Empatheatre is ultimately about questions such as: Where is home? What is home? Where do we belong? These questions seem to reverberate throughout *Isidlamlilo/The Fire Eater*.

Neil: Absolutely, as does the deeply loaded land question. Zenzile's story is so much about the yearning to return to paradise. This desperate urge to belong in the land of your ancestors, a land where you are free to move, to plant your own food and provide for your family. South Africa's past and current history is, tragically, one of so many paradises robbed and rubbished . . . so many communities moved and fractured.

Mpume: Although Zenzile has a yearning to leave the city and return to the rural area where she grew up, she is lost in a kind of childhood memory of that place. Throughout the play she informs us that her neighbours keep telling her that things have changed there, that the land has been sold off by the government, all the rivers have been polluted by factories and the valleys turned into landfills. I find it so sad to think that the Ipharadesi she remembers only really exists in her imagination. It's no longer the wild, magical place she experienced as a child.

Dylan: The visual sociology of this project was significant. This was the part that I was involved in the most, and I found it deeply inspiring and so rich in its own way as a research process. There was knowledge emergent in the 'making' of the set. Much care and time and imagination went into the set design led by Greg King and the lighting design by Tina le Roux. This play takes place in Zenzile's small hostel room, with the set based on images of the Thokoza hostel in Durban. Tell us more about the realism adopted in the design.

Neil: For the set, one of the first things we did was pore over photographer Angela Buckland's powerful photo essay on women living in Thokoza hostel, a body of work that captured the intimate details of various inhabitants' lives.[1] Our goal was to enable the audience to feel the smallness of the world that Zenzile has been forced to inhabit, and Greg King's set beautifully creates these limitations. This giant life, this operatic story, squeezed into a tiny matchbox.

Mpume: I spent time at Thokoza Women's Hostel and tried to memorise all the details of the place. The women are forced to live in very cramped, tiny spaces – literally concrete cubicles. We really wanted the audience to feel that intimacy in the storytelling and in the set design. I got to know a lot of the women in the hostel. These mamas were so much like the grandmothers in my own life, the women of my community in Umlazi. So many of the details of the set dressing I drew from my life, from my aunts and cousins, from my friends' parents' homes – and from the hostel. We had to get those details right: things like the kind of dishcloth she would use; the ritual of applying Vaseline after bathing at night; what would be in the cup at her bedside; the doily that her Bible would sit on.

Neil: Mpume really was the adviser on props and set details. It's amazing how many people walk out of the show afterwards and come tell us how it reminded them of their gogos, and of the domestic workers who raised them.

Mpume: Yes! People see their own grandparents sitting there.

Neil: The feeling that the space is authentic is very important to us as Empatheatre. Yet, within the 'kitchen sink realism' of Zenzile's room, there comes a whole lot of magical realism that unfolds throughout the play. For example, the rain on the window, the imagery of the lightning on her back, the scar and the tree. Zenzile speaks of her grandmother's monkey apple tree from Ipharadesi, the seed she plants, and the way she is able, within this forsaken concrete room, to keep a piece of Ipharadesi alive. It becomes a sign of hope at the end of the play.

Dylan: Yes, so much is reflected in the scar that is projected on her back, which is lightning, a scar and an upside-down tree of life.

Neil: As Empatheatre we always work carefully to craft and define a central image that pulls all the threads and symbols of the play together. To me, the scar is the central image of *Isidlamlilo/The Fire Eater*. The scar is used throughout the play to symbolise the vestiges of trauma and violence that mark many South Africans' bodies and lives. And while some characters in the play chose to interpret it as an evil omen or the wings of the lightning bird, Zenzile's grandmother is able to transform this painful mark into a sign of strength, referring to it as 'the tree of all life' and 'a river getting stronger and stronger with many, many smaller streams flowing into it'.

Mpume: Zenzile's grandmother sees this scar as an image of power and an image of healing, rather than just trauma. Scars are reminders of life for the gogo character – a reminder that we are still here. We made it through when others around us have not been as fortunate.

Dylan: Thinking of that tiny room, and how the audience is able to traverse with Zenzile the hills of the rural area of Ipharadesi, as well as the post-apocalyptic world that she inherits on the other side of the end of the world . . . how did you manage to bend space/time like this?

Mpume: I think what happens is I take myself through that journey. I see myself there, with my own eyes. When I am performing, I am not just saying lines; I am actively imagining each detail. I think that if I'm able to see it myself, then audience members can see it too, and they stay with me. If I don't hold those images in my mind, I could lose them. It's a very active thing. On a practical level it's finding comfortable ways to move and shift around the small area on stage. Neil and I worked carefully here, with the direction and blocking.

Dylan: Mpume, you often receive the response from sangomas and traditional healers/shamans watching your one-woman performances that you are in the company of others and that ancestors are with you when you are on stage. You also have stated openly that you are a sangoma who uses story and words as umuthi (sacred medicine). Could you share something more about this, and explain how *Isidlamlilo/The Fire Eater* is muthi for the audience?

Mpume: In this show and in others, people have said they can see that I am not alone on stage, that my ancestors are working through me, and it's true. On the set, in Zenzile's room, behind her bed there are photographs of her family stuck to the wall, but the truth is that those images are of my family, my grandmother in particular. I work with her in this performance. In some shows, I ask her to take over. I entrust the performance to her, and she works through me. Yes, my performance is my umuthi, and so it becomes umuthi for the audience, because it's sincere and very intimate. As I said earlier, I imagine each part of the story in my own mind so the audience can 'see' it with me. This is the same thing: the healing is real for me, and so it will be real for others.

Neil: With *Isidlamlilo/The Fire Eater*, I think we have seen how it's encouraging people to go home and have conversations. We keep getting feedback on how the play lives on inside people and in their relationships. I have heard of several people going home and asking their own grandmothers what their involvement was during the time of the IFP and ANC violence. And so, whether it's working at a higher level of policymaking or creating dialogue in kitchens and homes, it is making an impact.

Dylan: We have seen this with many Empatheatre productions: people sometimes take a few days before they even respond, and this feels even more heightened in the case of *Isidlamlilo/The Fire Eater*, because audiences say there's just so much to work through and process.

Neil: This is the most exciting of responses for us as writers and storytellers.

Dylan: I want to thank you both for reflecting with me today.

Mpume: It's been wonderful to talk about this play like this.

Neil: Thank you both for sharing your insights. It's really lovely to be able to unpack the work together in this way.

Note

1. Angela Buckland, Jo Lees and Melinda Silverman, 'Narratives of Home and Neighbourhood: Thokoza Women's Hostel', research report for the Urban Futures Centre, 2019, accessed 6 September 2023, https://narrativesofhome.org.za/wp-content/uploads/2019/08/Narratives-of-Home-Thokoza-Womens-Hostel.pdf.

Printed and bound by CPI Group (UK) Ltd, Croydon, CR0 4YY

25/03/2025

14647336-0001